What would you do in this situation?

You: (Insert your child's name here), put your shoes on before you go outside.

Child: I don't want to wear my shoes.

You: Put your shoes on.

Child: You're stupid and yucky.

You could:
1. Lose your temper
2. Ground the kid for a week
   or
3. Reach for *It's More Than Just Talk*

This invaluable book will show you how to effectively deal with behavioral problems such as the one above (an act of rebellion and defiance challenging your authority) and other situations that will inevitably come up in day-to-day life.

It's More Than Just Talk

ERIC & LINDA MATTHIESEN

Power Books
Fleming H. Revell Company
Old Tappan, New Jersey

Scripture quotations marked NIV are from the Holy Bible, New International Version. Copyright © 1973, 1978, 1984 International Bible Society. Used by permission of Zondervan Bible Publishers.

Scripture verse marked TLB is taken from *The Living Bible*, Copyright © 1971 by Tyndale House Publishers, Wheaton, Ill. Used by permission.

Material from PARENT EFFECTIVENESS TRAINING by Dr. Thomas Gordon copyright © 1970 by Thomas Gordon. Reprinted by permission of David McKay Co., a Division of Random House.

Quotation from "Parental Commitment Tied to Teens' Problems" by Norman Podhoretz, *Omaha World Herald*, reprinted with special permission of NAS, Inc.

Material adapted from *Family Forum* by Jay Kesler copyright © 1984, used by permission of Victor Books.

Material on reality discipline adapted from MAKING CHILDREN MIND WITHOUT LOSING YOURS by Dr. Kevin Leman copyright © 1984 by Dr. Kevin Leman. Used by permission of Fleming H. Revell Company.

Material adapted from HIDE OR SEEK by James Dobson copyright © 1974, 1979 by Fleming H. Revell Company. Used by permission of Fleming H. Revell Company.

Figure from FUNDAMENTAL CONCEPTS IN HUMAN COMMUNICATION by Ronald Applebaum, et al., copyright © 1973 by Ronald L. Applebaum, et al. Reprinted by permission of Harper & Row, Publisher, Inc.

Library of Congress Cataloging-in-Publication Data

Matthiesen, Eric.
    It's more than just talk : the art of communicating with your children / Eric and Linda Matthiesen.
        p.   cm.
    ISBN 0-8007-5325-9
    1. Parenting—United States. 2. Communication in the family–United States. 3. Parent and child—United States. 4. Parenting–Religious aspects—Christianity. 5. Values—Study and teaching–United States. I. Matthiesen, Linda. II. Title.
HQ755.8.M384 1989
306.874—dc20   89-8468
                                                         CIP

Copyright © 1989 by Eric and Linda Matthiesen
Published by the Fleming H. Revell Company
Old Tappan, New Jersey 07675
Printed in the United States of America

TO Keri and Jimmy
and
their grandmother Marion

Acknowledgments

Marion B. Matthiesen went to live with the Lord on March 20, 1984. She was sixty-four years old. Four months after her death, Holt International Children's Services referred Keri and Jimmy to us for adoption.

We remember our last visit with Eric's mother in December 1983. We sat at her dining room table writing our responses to seventeen pages of short-answer questions our agency would use to determine our suitability to be adoptive parents.

Eric's mother worked nearby—cooking, cleaning, sewing. Each time we completed a question, we would read aloud our answer. Each answer had to satisfy Mother. She wasn't taking any chances! Soon we were making fun of her editorial prerogative. Eric read the question, "What attracted you to your spouse?" and gave his answer: "I can't remember." We all laughed. We enjoyed sharing silly answers before reading what we had really written. But when we came to the question, "In what ways would you bring up your child as you were raised?" Eric played it straight. He read what he had written:

> Just as I was given ample affection and praise, I intend to support my child with ample love and affection. I also intend to provide the same quality of direction given me through clear rules and consistent enforcement of those rules.

   Much of what we seek to share in this book, Eric first learned from his mother. We are deeply indebted to her. We also are grateful to our friend Jim Karabatsos, who read the manuscript and contributed suggestions.

Contents

Introduction

Introducing Ourselves

We gazed out the open window into a world we did not know but in which we felt warmly welcome. Below us were small brick Korean homes, each surrounded by a small stone fence. Two or three large covered kimchee pots stood at each back door. We tried to focus our senses on the many unfamiliar smells and noises, but we couldn't concentrate.

We smiled nervously, holding hands and squeezing each other's fingers tightly, as if we were on a roller coaster inching our way toward that first plunge. Noises on the stairs. The door opened. At long last, there we stood, face-to-face.

It had been almost a year since we had taken the advice of Linda's father who, upon hearing of our adoption plans, made one response: "If you're going to get one, get two!" We thought about his advice, and it made sense. Each child would have a blood relative. We would avoid the "lonely only" syndrome characteristic of single-child families. And we could complete the adoption process in one step, avoiding having to reapply and face a long wait if children were unavailable.

Our three-year-old girl came through the door first, moving fast. She hit Linda like a freight train. She had a big smile and lots of kisses. Her two-year-old brother followed. Moving slowly but steadily, he crawled up on Eric's lap and flashed a big smile. The many letters and pictures we had sent them since receiving their pictures four months earlier had gotten through. Keri and Jimmy (we gave them American names) knew who we were, and they were happy to see us.

We spoke our first words to one another. Assuring Keri and Jimmy, "Sa-rang tang-sin" (We love you), we began our lifelong relationship. There were so many things to work out—our expectations, their expectations; what things meant to us, what things meant to them; our values, their values. Great differences divided us— differences in language, culture, age, and energy level. We were total strangers. But we had one thing going for us: We wanted it to work. We desperately wanted to be a family.

What We All Want

We were not unique in our deep desire to be a successful family. Everyone feels the same. *Every parent, every child, wants to relate as an effective family.* We are committed to the truth of this proposition. Toddlers, grade-schoolers, pre-adolescents, adolescents, young adults, middle-agers, and elderly persons—all are endowed with a deep-seated desire to establish and maintain a happy family life.

Despite these deep desires, few succeed. And why? Because wishing isn't enough. If they are to succeed, families need a plan and the communication skills to put that plan into effect.

Did you ever take a course in school called, "Building an Effective Family 101"? Probably not, because conventional wisdom says that effective family skills are supposed to be learned by example. It is modeled behavior.

Unfortunately, good models needed for learning effective family skills aren't present in every home. In fact, few homes are so blessed. American society has undergone dramatic changes since World War II. With increased affluence have come busier schedules, a mobile population, and the Me generation. Homes handicapped by the unhealthy effects of job pressures, television addiction, financial problems, and overcommitted parents often lack good role models needed to transmit effective family skills. So, what if you weren't blessed with a good role model?

Then you'll have to learn your family skills from this book and others like it. We had to do our homework, and we're still doing it. Our parents were loving and caring, and they provided for us well. But they were imperfect people. As we assumed our role as parents, there were gaps in our skills and abilities. So we compensated. We read a lot. We experimented. And although we remained imperfect, we got better.

What About This Book?

We have written this book to share our experience with you. We are not psychologists or family counselors. Eric teaches classes in interpersonal and group communication at the university level. Linda is a speech pathologist who teaches first- and second-grade language-delayed children. Operating within the limits of our expertise, we have tried to present the basic communication principles used by successful families. Our adoption required early identification and application of these principles. We had to establish effective communication with our children, and we had to teach Keri and Jimmy to communicate effectively with us. These are two problems all families face. Communication is a complex process, and mistakes are commonplace.

In the following pages we hope to help you sharpen your communication skills. We offer suggestions for building those skills in your children.

Acquiring and applying the principles we present is a continuous process. Some days you'll struggle. You'll want to take back your words, change your timing, or use a whole different set of nonverbals. But communication is irreversible. So you'll take a deep breath, exhale slowly, and say under your breath, "Next time I'll do it better!" Other days you'll be soaring! You'll manage your communication about as well as is humanly possible.

As you try to communicate effectively with your children, your relationship with them will become the rich and rewarding experience God meant it to be.

A Parent's Prayer

Lord, don't let me make a mess of things.
Psalms 119:31 TLB

PART I
THE PARENT-CHILD COMMUNICATION PUZZLE

The three chapters that form Part I lay out the principles of effective communication. The first chapter, "Using Effective Verbal Messages: The Right Mix," closely examines the fabric that is the substance of our messages. Chapter 1 introduces parents to six types of statements used in parent/child communication. Just as knowledge of various fabrics, their price, and where they can be obtained enables the seamstress to sew quality garments, knowledge of the various statements parents can make to their children will enable you to establish and maintain a rewarding relationship with your children.

Chapter 2, "Using Effective Nonverbal Messages: Great Performances," stresses the importance of attached messages. Our use of voice, manner, and space greatly affects the meaning children assign to the words we speak.

Chapter 3, "Being a Parent Who Understands the Communication Process," provides an overview of how communication works. This chapter highlights the components of the communication process and the characteristics of family communication.

1
Using Effective Verbal Messages: The Right Mix

A word aptly spoken is like apples of gold in settings of silver.

Proverbs 25:11 NIV

A Format for Parental Communication

Imagine what would happen if you recorded everything you said for a week. You probably would find that you speak more than fifty thousand words a day. What do you suppose you say using all those words?

"Well," you might speculate, "I probably give over a hundred directives a day, telling the kids to brush their teeth, take the dog out, that kind of thing. And let's see, I'll bet I ask for information at least five hundred times a day, saying things like, 'Kids, did you brush your teeth and take the dog out?' Golly, I don't know what kind of statements I make using all those words. What difference does it make, anyway?"

It makes a big difference! Knowing the types of messages you send each day enables you to better manage your family relationships. By identifying the types of messages you send, you can ask yourself, "What are my options? Which message(s) will best strengthen the relationship I enjoy with my children?"

Identifying the types of messages you send sounds like a complicated, technical job, but it really isn't. Believe it or not, it's a lot like making cookies. Communication researchers treat all the statements you make in a day the way a baker treats cookie dough. They roll out the dough on an imaginary table and look around for some cookie cutters. Each cookie cutter should be different (communication researchers want unique cookies), and together the cookie cutters should cut all the dough (communication researchers don't want any leftovers). When they find the cookie cutters that satisfy these two requirements, they arrange them on the dough and cut their cookies.

Communication professionals commonly use five cookie cutters to identify the types of messages people send.[1] We'll add a sixth cookie cutter, taken from the Bible, to form our framework for examining parent/child communication. You will encounter these six cookie cutters again and again throughout this book. Here, then, are six types of messages that affect parent/child relationships:

Description Statements

Description statements consist of the information that comes to you through your senses: what you see, hear, touch, feel, and smell. Pure description statements mirror the images produced by a camera or the sounds saved by a tape recorder. They are objective. Description statements don't go beyond the experience that the speaker seeks to share. They are free of interpretation.

That sounds simple enough, but description statements are difficult to formulate because most people have a difficult time separating their inferences from their observations. We have learned to go beyond the facts of an event and to infer the many things the facts imply. Making these inferences does not in itself lead to trouble, but our tendency to regard inferences as facts does. And the tendency toward inference/observation confusion is almost universal—just about everybody makes this mistake.

"Me? Not me!" you reply. Yes, you. And here's proof. Read the following short story and decide whether the five statements at the end are true, false, or neither true nor false (can't tell).

> Two boys go downstairs. A door slams shut. The water in the bathroom begins running. One boy says, "Be careful! You're going to spill some." One boy comes upstairs with a wet shirt.
> 1. Two boys go to the basement. (True) (False) (Can't Tell)
> 2. The bathroom door slams shut. (True) (False) (Can't Tell)
> 3. Downstairs, water begins running. (True) (False) (Can't Tell)
> 4. Somebody spills water. (True) (False) (Can't Tell)
> 5. One boy is wearing a wet shirt. (True) (False) (Can't Tell)[2]

If you answered true or false for any of these statements, you made an error. All five statements are inferences and should be answered as neither true nor false. Each statement goes beyond the facts presented in the story.

Statement 1 has the boys going to the basement. True, we were told the boys went downstairs; however, the boys might have been going from the second floor to the first floor. We don't know if they were using the basement stairs. Statement 2 has a bathroom door slamming shut, but the story simply said, "A door slams shut." Statement 3 places the running water downstairs while the story merely said, "Water begins running in the bathroom." That bathroom need not be a downstairs bathroom. Water could have started running in a second-story bathroom. Statement 4 has somebody spilling water when the story never said any water was spilled. Finally, statement 5 has one boy wearing a wet shirt when the story had one boy coming upstairs with a wet shirt. The boy in the story could have been wearing the shirt or he could have been carrying it.

If you missed a few, don't feel bad. Most people confuse their inferences with their facts. Actually, correcting the tendency toward inference/observation confusion is easy. It merely requires that you follow a few rules suggested by communication experts:[3] First, *label your inferences.* Say to yourself, "Is what I am thinking inference or fact?" "How do I know *X, Y,* or *Z?* "Have I inferred these things?" "Have I observed these things?" Then *calculate the risk.* Ask yourself, "If my inference is incorrect and I act on it as if it were fact or I relate it to another person as if it were fact, what could be the consequences?" "What do I or what does someone else have to lose if my inference is wrong?" And finally, *disclose your inferences.* Tell your listeners that what you've said is something you have inferred.

Suppose Keri and Jimmy went downstairs. Then suppose Linda heard a door slam and water start running, and so on. Then Jimmy came upstairs with a wet shirt. Linda could respond with a pure description statement by saying, "You and Keri went downstairs, I heard water running in the house, and I see that shirt is wet."

Chances are Jimmy would supply the missing information, especially if it incriminated his sister. And Jimmy should have a chance to explain—a chance he wouldn't have gotten if Linda had said, "I told you not to play with the water in the downstairs bathroom. Now you've spilled water on your shirt and on the floor. You're always into mischief."

Inference/observation confusion undermines many relationships. As parents, we would be wise to heed the Bible's warning against falling into its trap: "What you have seen with your eyes do not bring hastily to court, for what will you do in the end if your neighbor puts you to shame?" (Proverbs 25:8 NIV).

Interpretation Statements

Unlike description statements, which merely report our experiences, interpretation statements comment on our experiences. They disclose what we think about a child's behavior. These thoughts are a product of our total personality.

The interpretative thoughts of a healthy and mature person contain two positive characteristics: (1) labeled inferences and (2) nonevaluative language. These positive characteristics give rise to what we have termed *functional interpretation statements*. On the other hand, the interpretive thoughts of an unhealthy or immature person contain two negative characteristics: (1) unlabeled inferences and (2) evaluative language. These negative characteristics produce what we have termed *dysfunctional interpretation statements*.

If Linda were an unhealthy or immature person, she would have responded to the wet shirt incident with dysfunctional interpretative statements like these:

"Jimmy, you're always into trouble. This morning you were playing with the telephone; now you're playing with water."

"Every time I let you go downstairs without me you get into trouble."

Notice how these two statements use the facts of Linda's past experiences to go beyond the facts of her present experience, and also how these statements label Jimmy's behavior as "tiring" and "annoying."

Here are two more examples of dysfunctional statements Linda could have made:

"The rule is no playing with water, and I expect you to obey the rule."

"I don't think you need to act like a baby to get the attention you want."

Notice how these statements use Linda's expectations to go beyond the facts of her present experience, and also how these statements label Jimmy's behavior as "disappointing" or "childish."

These examples illustrate the disadvantages of dysfunctional interpretation statements. Such statements confuse inference with fact. The above four examples imply that Jimmy was playing with water when Linda didn't know that was true. Dysfunctional interpretation statements also contain implicit and/or explicit put-downs. All the above examples are judgmental. Put yourself in Jimmy's shoes. If someone talked to you as illustrated in the above examples, wouldn't you be likely to become rebellious and defensive?

Fortunately, healthy and mature persons can formulate functional interpretation statements by labeling the inferences they make and avoiding evaluative language. Because Linda is a healthy and mature person, she would have responded to Jimmy by using the following functional interpretation statements:

"I am just guessing, but I think your shirt got wet because you were playing with water."

"I think you were playing with water because I heard water running downstairs."

Feeling Statements

Feeling statements disclose your emotional state. They reflect your private thoughts and moods. Feeling statements objectify these private thoughts and moods so they can be shared with others. In some ways, they are like description statements in that they don't go beyond the experience the speaker seeks to communicate. They are free of interpretation.

The ability to formulate effective feeling statements greatly determines the quality of parent/child relationships. Effective feeling statements enable children to establish and maintain an appropriate orientation to their parents. By expressing effective feeling statements, children can locate their parents on a map of human moods. In a sense, these statements allow children to take our emotional temperature. Understanding our emotional state enables children to enact appropriate behaviors toward us. This puts them at ease and increases their confidence when relating to us. No child likes to relate to a parent who is an enigma.

Unfortunately, most parents don't share their feelings well. Most parental communication consists largely of description and interpretation statements. Infrequent and ineffective emotional expression is evidenced by our weak emotional vocabularies. When asked to come up with a list of words describing various emotional states, most of us are hard-pressed to describe more than a few basic feelings. Take a moment and try it. See how many single words you can name that describe the various shades of just three basic emotions: happy, sad, and angry.

Now check your list against the one below to see which ones you overlooked.

Feelings

Happy	Sad	Angry
beaming	broody	acerbated
buoyant	cheerless	chafed
chipper	dejected	cranky

congenial	disconsolate	enraged
delighted	distressed	exasperate
effervescent	doleful	fiery
exhilarated	forlorn	fuming
frolicsome	gloomy	furious
gay	grieving	galled
genial	heartbroken	grouchy
glad	inconsolable	hot
gleeful	joyless	incensed
jolly	melancholy	infuriated
jovial	miserable	irate
lively	mournful	irritated
merry	pensive	mad
mirthful	rueful	miffed
pleasant	somber	provoked
rapturous	sorrowful	raging
rosy	sorry	riled
smiling	tristful	sore
solaced	wailful	testy
sunny	weeping	vexed
winsome	woeful	wrathful

In addition to using single words to express their feelings, parents frequently use expressive phrases: "I'm walking on air," "I feel super," or "I feel like dancing." These expressions are useful, but too often sentences that contain the words *I feel* sound like emotional expression when, in fact, such statements express intentions or thoughts. The statement "I feel like taking the kids to the park" sounds as if it contains an emotional component, but it is actually a statement of intention. Here's another pseudoemotional statement: "Keri, I feel you've been picking on Jimmy." This emotional-sounding statement is really expressing an opinion. Often parents think they are communicating emotions when they're not. As parents, we fool ourselves into thinking we've provided enough emotional content for our children to identify our moods and respond appropriately, when we really have been expressing only our intentions and opinions.

The truth is that most of us are unable to express our emotions effectively. This shortcoming comes as no surprise when we look at our subdued society. The expression of strong emotion is discouraged in our homes, schools, and businesses. Children have few role models when it comes to expressing strong emotions. Instead, authority figures often discourage emotional expression:

"Hold your temper."

"You shouldn't feel bad."

"Settle down, you're too excited."

"That's not funny."

These restrictive phrases serve to prepare us for employment. In order for us to assume positions in the workplace, we must display emotional restraint. Salespeople, waiters, and receptionists must always be pleasant and helpful. We expect doctors and their colleagues in the health care field to remain objective and dispassionate even when communicating tragic news.

And so we learn to avoid disclosing how we feel. Instead, we develop and project an image consistent with how we believe others expect us to feel. After all, a true statement of our feelings could lead to embarrassment. After years of restraining our emotions, we eventually lose the ability to even recognize our feelings. The feelings are there, but we don't attend to them, so we fail to express them. Our emotions stay inside us and never serve us or our children.

Forgiving Statements

Forgiving statements consist of words that release children from guilt and shame and release parents from anger and resentment. Author Archibald Hart defines *forgiveness* as giving up our right to hurt another for hurting us. Because most children operate from a self-centered perspective and struggle with rebellion, parents often have a daily need to deliver forgiving statements.

Humanistic communication scholars have little to say on the subject, but the Bible directly addresses the need for forgiveness. Repeatedly, the Bible makes two important points that parents should heed.

First, forgive as often as your children need forgiveness: "If your brother sins, rebuke him, and if he repents, forgive him. If he sins against you seven times in a day, and seven times comes back to you and says, 'I repent,' forgive him" (Luke 17:3, 4 NIV).

Second, don't harbor your anger: "'In your anger do not sin': Do not let the sun go down while you are still angry, and do not give the devil a foothold" (Ephesians 4:26, 27 NIV).

Eric's mother would reply, "Sorry doesn't help!" when her children came to apologize for mischief, sassy talk, or irresponsibility. Maybe she felt she was being manipulated by insincere apologies, or perhaps she had just hit bottom and was fed up with having to cope with difficult children.

We hope you will never tell your children that "sorry doesn't help," because "sorry" does help. It helps the relationship between parents and children. It clears the air, dispelling the damaging emotions of guilt and anger.

Keri and Jimmy once scribbled with their crayons on our living room couch. After disciplining them, Eric accepted their apologies with the following forgiving statements: "Everybody makes mistakes, and your mistakes do not change our love for you. Your mother and I forgive you. The scribbling on the living room couch is forgotten, and we'll not bring it up again."

Effect Statements

Effect statements explain the impact of a specific behavior. They help children understand the implications of their behavior. We use effect statements to focus on how the child's behavior impacts on us, himself, and/or others.

"When you didn't tell me you were going next door to play [description statement], I couldn't find you and I spent an hour searching the neighborhood for you [effect statement]. I was afraid something awful had happened to you [feeling statement]."

"When you eat only the meat on your plate [description statement], you don't get the carbohydrates, minerals, and vitamins you need for adequate growth [effect statement]. I am worried what will happen if you don't eat a balanced meal [feeling statement]."

"I don't think you wanted to hurt Jimmy [interpretation statement], but when you told your brother he couldn't play with you and your friends [description statement], Jimmy thought you didn't like him anymore [effect statement]."

We often assume that our children are aware of the consequences of their behavior and don't need to be told. Unfortunately, frequently children are unaware of the effects of their behavior. Not knowing what they've done makes it difficult for them to understand what is bothering us. We need to use effect statements to provide kids with the background they need to accept our feeling statements.

Result Statements

Result statements disclose to your children how you are predisposed to act. Like feeling statements, result statements are the product of our total personality. Our countless past experiences produce the beliefs, opinions, values, and attitudes that govern our behavior.

Beliefs   Beliefs consist of statements we accept as true. Our meaning system contains tens of thousands of beliefs. We hold beliefs about unique experiences such as our private fears or our personal encounters with God. We hold beliefs about our identity, who and what we are. We hold beliefs about authority figures, who to believe and who to ignore. We hold a wide range of beliefs derived from authority figures, everything from what is fashionable dress to what foods are nutritious. And we hold many inconsequential beliefs, such as which deodorant best stops wetness or what color car is most attractive.

Opinions   Opinions consist of the beliefs that we voice publicly. Because of their public nature, opinions are largely socially determined. We are prone to say what is expected and accepted by others. Opinions are unreliable indicators of our real beliefs.

Values   Values consist of statements we accept as good and positive, as well as true. Compared with our beliefs and opinions, we hold relatively few values. The values we do hold, however, tend to endure over the years and are internally consistent. Our values change, but they do so slowly. Our values rarely are inconsistent. For example, it is unlikely that we would place an equal value on family and self-indulgence.

Attitudes   Attitudes are predispositions to behave in a certain manner. In a way, we use our attitudes to program ourselves to act in accordance with our beliefs and values.

Here's how the process works: Suppose Jimmy begins a period of testing our rules. Linda experiences Jimmy's defiance. After a while, she forms several beliefs about Jimmy's behavior: (1) Jimmy is testing our rules. (2) Jimmy has been testing them for three days. (3) Consistent enforcement of the rules has not reduced his tendency to test. (4) I am getting tired of his relentless defiance. (5) The situation is becoming intolerable. (6) If Jimmy defies me one more time, it will be terrible. (7) Since it will be terrible if Jimmy defies me again, I must not allow it to happen.

These seven beliefs then coalesce to form an attitude that will predispose Linda to act in a certain way if Jimmy tests again. The attitude Linda adopts might be general and indefinite: If Jimmy tests one more rule, I'll teach him a lesson he won't forget. Or Linda's attitude might be specific and definite: The next time Jimmy tests a rule, I am going to make him sit on a chair for three minutes. Either way, Linda is preprogrammed! Jimmy doesn't know she is ready to take action, but Linda is cocked and set to fire.

Result statements enable us to inform our children how we are likely to act in response to their behavior. Suppose in response to Jimmy's testing behavior, Linda had been reminding him of the rules he was breaking. Since Jimmy is not a mind reader, he would have no way of knowing that Linda now was predisposed to act in a different way, having formed a new attitude. Unless Linda used a result statement to communicate her planned actions, Jimmy would find himself being disciplined without the opportunity to decide if the consequences of continued testing were acceptable. Rightly or wrongly, Jimmy could regard discipline under these circumstances as unfair. All this unpleasantness could be avoided, however, if Linda were to make the following response:

"That's the third time this morning you've broken our rules for playing in the house [description statement]. I am wondering if you're interested in seeing how many rules

you can break before I take action [interpretation state-
ment]. I just want you to know I am getting tired of the
rules being broken [feeling statement]. Every time you
break a rule, I have to stop working and remind you how
to behave [effect statement]. The next time you break a
rule this morning, I am going to put you on a chair for
three minutes [result statement]."

DIFFER

The DIFFER format—Description-Interpretation-Feeling-Forgiving-Effect-Result—enables parents to formulate
messages that promote healthy family relationships. Children relate better to parents who disclose their interpretations, share their feelings, discuss the effects of the child's
behavior, and make known the actions they will take if the
child persists in that behavior. Children can orient themselves easily to such fully communicating parents. They
know where they stand and what their parents are likely to
do next. That's all any kid wants. Tragically, few kids enjoy
effective parental communication.

Instead, the world communicates with its children using
evaluative language, inaccurate language, inaccurate interpretations, hidden feelings, and inadequate explanation. Paul admonishes Christians to reject the common
practices of the world: "Do not conform any longer to the
pattern of this world, but be transformed by the renewing
of your mind" (Romans 12:2 NIV).

DIFFER provides Christian parents with a biblically
based alternative communication style. We urge you to
commit yourself to learning this more effective approach
to parent-child communication.

It won't be easy. If you're like us, you will have many
old habits to break. But we've seen substantial gains made
in a short period of time by those who live by Paul's

refusal to accept human limitations: "I can do everything through him who gives me strength" (Philippians 4:13 NIV).

You can begin by following four basic principles of DIFFER.

DIFFER Tutorial

---

1. *Be yourself.* Word your statements as you now talk and converse. Be true to your present style of language use. Instead of saying, "As a consequence of your behavior," say something that feels genuine to you. You might feel more comfortable saying something like, "Since I had to wait an hour for you. . . ."

2. *Be flexible.* The acronym DIFFER is nothing more than a mnemonic to help you remember the six elements that comprise the communication format we recommend. Frequently, the order implied by this acronym is an effective sequence in which to organize your messages. But there is nothing wrong with arranging your statements in some other order. In the following chapters you'll see examples where we have deviated from the order implied by the acronym because we believed the alternative order strengthened the communication.

3. *Be concise.* Combine statements where possible. For example, you might say, "After I saw that the dishes weren't washed, I began to worry that you had broken our agreement." This message contains description, effect, and interpretation statements.

4. *Be strategic.* Successful communication requires making effective choices. You can never say everything you know or feel. Time constraints and unattentive listeners are just two of the reasons we can't say everything we have to say. As a result, we must restrict and focus on the statements that will most effectively evoke the meanings we want to share.

We solve this problem by first discovering what we *might* say and then choosing carefully the things we *will* say. DIFFER is a format that continually puts your options before you. You always know you have six statements from which to choose, but you don't have to choose all six. Sometimes the situation allows you to use only one or two.

We know that having a strategy is not always possible in the thick of family life. But when the situation permits advance planning, take the time, even if it is only a matter of a few seconds.

Part II of this book applies the DIFFER format to the problem of establishing and maintaining effective family relationships. You will learn how to use DIFFER to manage discipline, self-esteem, intimacy, conflict resolution, and education and instruction.

2
Using Effective Nonverbal Messages: Great Performances

A servant cannot be corrected by mere words;
though he understands, he will not respond.

Proverbs 29:19 NIV

Here is a typical conversation you're likely to overhear at our house:

Keri: We *never* get to go to the videotape store. We *never* get to see our favorite shows.

Linda: That's because I don't want you watching television all the time. You have tons of toys that you never play with. Besides, you belong outside on a nice day like today.

Keri: I don't want to play outside.

Linda: Okay, then play in your room or downstairs.

Keri: (*in a whiny voice*) But I want to go to the videotape store.

Linda: I said no, and I mean NO! Now go and play nicely.

Keri: (*as she disappears down the stairs*) It's not fair!

Sound familiar? Such everyday conversations are so much a part of the fabric of our lives that we rarely pay much attention to them. And that's too bad, because a close examination of what goes on between ourselves and our children can improve our ability to be effective parents.

When we exchange verbal messages, nonverbal messages often accompany the words we speak. We emit the two messages simultaneously. For example, had you seen Keri responding to Linda's refusal to take her to the videotape store, you would have observed her folding her arms, leaning back on one foot, and heaving a big sigh after muttering, "It's not fair," under her breath.

The Elements of Nonverbal Communication

By nonverbal communication we mean those messages expressed by means other than the use of language. Parents and children use a wide range of behaviors to express messages without the use of language.

Touch

One researcher notes that "skin is the first and most powerful medium of communication."[1] We touch our children a lot. At the breakfast table, we hug them when we put them in their booster chairs, we kiss them after we've tied their bibs, we hold hands during grace, we squeeze the backs of their necks if we're going to the refrigerator to get more milk. We stay in touch! In addition to touching our children, we touch each other in front of our children. We hold hands when we walk together, we put our arms around each other when we're watching television, we hug and kiss when we leave for work and when we come home.

The importance of touching has been firmly established. Ashley Montagu has demonstrated that a number of health problems are caused by lack of infant-mother contact.[2] Some studies show that high levels of physical stimulation are associated with higher IQs. Children who lack physical stimulation fail to develop to their full potential.[3] And so we touch our kids a lot. But equally important to Keri and Jimmy's physical health are the effects of touch on their mental health. Our frequent physical contact carries a message of acceptance. Touching reinforces our words of affection and love and builds self-esteem.

How do the kids respond to all this touching? They give us back a great deal of physical contact. They take our hands when we're walking. Jimmy pats Eric on the back at 3:00 A.M. when being carried to the toilet. They stroke our ears when we nap together. And we love it. We come away feeling good about our sacrifices for them. Suddenly, it's all worthwhile.

Eye Contact

Eyes lay the foundation for relational communication. Hence, eye contact is critical to communication between parents and children. When we want to speak with our children, we first engage their eyes. This action announces to them our readiness to communicate. Just saying their names, followed by a pause, usually results in gaining eye contact. When they are excited or distracted, however, it is often necessary to issue a simple directive before speaking, such as, "Keri, look at me." Mutual eye contact indicates that both child and parent are ready to exchange language messages.

Use of Space

Parents and children relate to one another using four categories of distance: intimate, personal, social, and public.

Intimate Distance Starting from our skins, intimate distance extends to about eighteen inches. Most communication with children under three years of age occurs within the intimate zone. Small children enjoy the freedom to move in and out of the intimate range. In unfamiliar situations, such as meeting new people, toddlers will often cling to their parents' legs. In the company of their friends, small children will zip in and out of the intimate zone as if to say, "This is my daddy and mommy, and they love me a lot. See, I can move in and out of their intimate zone anytime I want."

Personal Distance This zone ranges from eighteen inches to about four feet. Most communication with children three to eight years of age occurs within the personal zone. It is from this distance that parents issue directives, ask questions, and get answers. Parents like to stay in this zone when disciplining their children, for they can command their attention and avoid being ignored when they move in this close. After they've "talked tough," Dad and Mom can move into the intimate zone to comfort and reassure their children.

Social Distance Beginning where the personal zone left off (about four feet), this zone extends to about twelve feet. The activities that take place in this zone usually involve supervision and conversation. Older children operate largely out of this zone, although they make use of the previous two zones as well.

Public Distance Public distance extends from twelve feet to whatever distance our voices will travel. Not much takes place between parents and children at this distance. Perhaps you have called your child at this distance, only to be ignored. Given the opportunity, you would probably prefer to move closer to your child before attempting communication.[4]

Parents and children also use space to establish territoriality. We occupy territory to reflect our status. That's why it is important that children have a place of their own, even if it is only a box or a shelf. Their right to privacy should be respected. We emphasize the need to knock before opening a closed door, and we adhere to the rule when entering Jimmy's or Keri's room.

Vocalizations

The qualities of voice include tone, speed, pitch, number and length of pauses, volume, and fluency. Research shows that mothers can distinguish among five different messages—hunger, fatigue, sleepiness, pain, or uneasiness—in the crying of two-week-old babies.[5] Parents combine the vocal qualities to form a paralanguage with which they can attach additional messages to their words. Sarcasm illustrates how parents attach messages to negate or even contradict their words.

When Linda wishes to communicate that she means business, she stresses the letter *t* with articulation, lower pitch, and increased volume. Her messages sound something like, "Sit down right now!" Jimmy's and Keri's compliance increases when Linda is pushing her *t*'s. On the other hand, when Keri increases her volume to repeat a question or statement to which we have responded, she is signaling to us that she thinks we have not understood her.

Body Orientation

The degree to which children face their parents signals their interest in interacting with them. When we discipline Jimmy, he often transmits his dislike for our message by turning away. This behavior goes beyond avoiding eye contact. Jimmy turns his whole body so we are talking to his ears. If Keri and Linda are working on a puzzle and Jimmy joins them, Keri frequently will turn away from Jimmy so that when she talks to him she almost has to talk over her shoulder. Her silent message is, "Go away. I was here first."

Facial Expressions

The face can produce a seemingly endless array of expressions. Researchers have identified eight distinguishable positions of the eyebrows and forehead, eight additional positions of the eyes and lids, and ten for the lower face. Acting together, these three variables alone can produce 640 different expressions. Add the distinguishable expressions of the remaining facial features—the mouth, nose, and cheeks, for example—and the number of possible expressions grows beyond identification and description.[6] Children communicate satisfaction or dissatisfaction through facial expressions. Parents should note that expert opinion regards the smile as one of the principal mechanisms for socialization and the development of effective interpersonal relations.[7] Proverbs 15:30 NIV declares, "A cheerful look brings joy to the heart, and good news gives health to the bones."

Gestures

Gestures refer to the movement of our hands, legs, and feet. They are a good source of nonverbal communication because few people try to mask their gestures. Most people work hard to control their facial expressions, but few people remember that their gestures are also communicating their feelings. Parents learn to read their children's gestures. Children telegraph their need to go to the toilet by touching themselves or jumping up and down on one foot. Jimmy tells us he is tired by increasing his body movements. It is as if he knows he'll fall asleep if he sits still, so he swings his legs or shakes his hand to stay awake. These gestures tell us when to end a story and announce, "It's bedtime."

Posture

The degree to which we sit and stand erect and the amount of tension with which we carry our bodies closely correlates with our true feelings of interest and involvement as well as confidence and determination. But often we fail to observe posture; instead we focus on competing nonverbals such as facial expressions and gestures. This is a mistake because posture reveals so much about the feelings of others.

Eric uses Keri's and Jimmy's posture to gauge their determination when they object to his directive or request his permission. Wouldn't it be wonderful if children were perfectly compliant! Imagine how simple family life would be if parents could order their children around the way a sergeant orders a private or a supervisor orders a subordinate. Of course, the reality is that children can't be court-martialed or fired, so they resist a directive they don't like. Consequently, Eric has learned to pick his fights carefully, avoiding confrontations over issues for which Keri and Jimmy exhibit determination. Before issuing a directive or refusing a request, Eric reads their posture. Are they going to take this lying down, or are they going to stand up and fight? Are they rigid and tense or loose and relaxed? It makes a difference.

Conduct

In addition to using body language, children and parents often resort to acting out their feelings. Frequently, children will use disruptive behavior to mask what they are feeling. Shortly after arriving home from kindergarten one day, Jim wandered through the living room while Eric was practicing the piano. Thinking that he was looking for something to do, Eric asked Jim if he would like to hear a new song he was learning. Jim said no, so Eric asked Keri, who said yes. Eric and Keri started singing while Eric played the piano. Jim left the room and returned with his toy guns, asking if Eric wanted to play GI Joe. Eric explained that he was busy at the piano but would play when he was finished. Keri and Eric continued singing the same song over and over, trying to get it right. Jim stepped up and hit Eric in the back as hard as he could. Message: "You're leaving me out! I can't play the piano and I can't read the words of the song. I found your asking me to join you frustrating. All your invitation did was remind me of my inadequacies, and I am good and mad about it!"

Acting out does not always involve disruptive behavior, particularly when a child wants to disclose rather than hide his feelings. One morning while sitting at the breakfast table, Keri picked up a full gallon jug of milk and poured it herself for the first time. Feeling a sense of accomplishment, she blurted out, "Did you see me pour my own milk!" Jim, seeing her accomplishment, took his bowl (from which he had eaten all the cereal but left most of the milk) to the sink. He proceeded to pour the remaining milk down the drain (about two cups). When he returned to the table, he said, "I want more cereal." He filled his bowl with Rice Krispies, reached for the full gallon jug of milk, and poured it into his bowl. Message: "I can pour my own milk, too!"

Nonverbal Communication in Children

As adults, parents often see early childhood as a time of bliss, joy, and laughter. Yet, it's not easy being a kid. For one thing, young children must struggle to make themselves understood. Babies have a great deal to say but no language with which to say it. Mothers compensate by developing supersensitive antennae for picking up nonverbal messages in order to better meet their babies' needs.

For example, suppose a mother puts her baby in his high chair while she fixes lunch. She gives him his favorite squeaky toy. He accepts the toy but then throws it across the room. Mother gets squeaky and puts it back in baby's hand. He gives it another toss. Mother thinks, *Boy, are you a grumpy bear today*, but then she notices the spoon she left on the kitchen table just a few inches out of his reach. She gives baby the spoon and presto, successful communication occurs.

Children's Encoding

These same powers of observation are needed to deal successfully with young children whose ability to encode their thoughts and feelings—that is, put their thoughts and feelings into messages—are just emerging.

Research suggests important age differences in the ability to encode feelings. Toddlers appear to express happy and sad feelings as accurately as do older children, such as fifth graders. However, the ability of children to accurately express feelings of anger and surprise seems heavily dependent on their age, improving with each year up to the age of eleven. Interestingly, it appears that fear is not accurately expressed even by older children, such as fifth graders.[8]

These research findings suggest that parents should carefully monitor their children for feelings of anger and fear. Younger children, in particular, need to be watched for feelings of anger and encouraged to express anger appropriately. After being falsely accused by Eric of hiding one of Jim's toys, Keri withdrew to her room. Upon learning of Keri's innocence, Eric entered her room to apologize. There was Keri, in bed and under the covers. Their conversation went like this:

Eric: Nobody likes to be blamed for something she didn't do.

Keri: I didn't hide Jimmy's toy.

Eric: I know that now, and I'm sorry I didn't take the time to find out all the facts.

Keri: You just said I did it.

Eric: I know. How did you feel when I said you took his toy?

Keri: Bad!

Eric: If I were your pillow, what would you do if I said you hid Jimmy's toy and you didn't?

Keri: (takes the pillow and spanks it)

Eric: You sure are angry, aren't you?

Keri: Ya.

Eric: It's okay to be angry, but since you can't spank me, how can you show me you're angry?

Keri: (holds up the pillow and makes an angry face)

Eric: Good job of letting me know your feelings.

While children develop encoding skills as they grow up, boys and girls differ in their ability to put specific feelings into messages. Generally, girls are better at expressing sad feelings while boys are better at expressing mad feelings. Wise parents will take these differences into account, watching their daughters for angry feelings and taking time to teach the expression of anger, as illustrated above.

Parents' Decoding

The most frustrating characteristic of nonverbal communication is the fact that unspoken messages are ambiguous. Of course, spoken messages are also ambiguous. For example, if Eric tells Keri to keep the sand in the sandbox and she replies, "Don't worry," is he to assume she has promised to do as he asked? What does "Don't worry" mean? That's hard to say, but not as hard as deciding what it means if Keri nods her head or just waves her hand in response to Eric's directive to keep the sand in the sandbox.

Parents with strong decoding skills (the ability to accurately attribute messages to behavior) are at an advantage in relating to their children. Being able to recognize your child's feelings enables you to be more empathic, which promotes the well-being and health of your child. Moreover, accurate decoding of your child's nonverbal communication enables you to help him name and interpret his feelings.[9]

Not all expressions of feeling are easily decoded, however. One study indicates that parents with low decoding skills have difficulty detecting spontaneously produced expressions of anger.[10] More encouragingly, the same study indicates that adults can accurately decode happiness and sadness.

How about your decoding skills? If you are a woman, chances are you are better than the average man at decoding nonverbal expressions.[11] If you are the parent of only girls, you probably are better at decoding nonverbal expressions in your children than are the parents of boys.[12] Unfortunately, few studies have examined how to improve the decoding skills of parents. Only the most global advice is presently available.

Trying to interpret nonverbal messages requires that you take into account three factors: *the context,* including the location, time, and situation (for example, your child rubbing his eyes at nine o'clock at night signals something different from your child rubbing his eyes after you've told him a story he can't believe); *the relationship between you and your child;* and *the emotional state of parent and child* (an angry child, frustrated by a broken toy, emits hostile nonverbals toward parents with whom he is not angry).

You also should try to take the role of the child in understanding what he or she might be feeling. Try to see things from the child's point of view. For example, both Keri and Jimmy frequently neglect to flush the toilet. From an adult perspective, their action suggests they are just lazy kids who won't take the time to be responsible. Keri and Jimmy's point of view presents a very different perspective. To them, toilets make a loud noise when flushed. Since they view the toilet as a threatening object, their failure to flush might be conduct that suggests they are acting out their fears. The following conversation would bring their fears to the surface:

Eric: Jimmy, come flush the toilet.

Jimmy: No, I'm too busy.

Eric: Come on, it will only take a minute.

Jimmy: Oh, okay. Why does it make so much noise (*said as he flushes*)?

Eric: The toilet can be scary to flush. Let me show you how it works (*Eric lifts the tank lid for a short demonstration*).

Parents' Encoding

Oddly enough, while most parents understand the nonverbal messages their children send, they are often unaware of their own nonverbal behavior. Take a few minutes to answer these questions:

1. How do you nonverbally tell your children you love them?
2. What nonverbals do you use to tell your children you are about to take disciplinary action?
3. What nonverbal messages do you send to tell your children you are tired and don't want to be bothered?
4. How do you nonverbally tell your children that "no" means NO!

"Oh," you might say, "when I communicate about these matters, I use words. I don't send many nonverbal messages." Wrong. You can't avoid communicating nonverbally. Go ahead and try it. Sit perfectly still. Don't look up. Keep your eyes on this book. Now, if someone walks into the room and sees you, what is the message he is likely to get? "I am busy reading, don't bother me." So you tried hard not to, but you still communicated.

"Hey, no fair," you might say, "I wasn't trying to communicate anything." True, but your intentions don't count. Someone assigned meaning to your behavior, and communication occurred. And what's more, many other unintended messages were probably received. How were you sitting? Was your posture erect, or were you relaxed and at ease? What about your face? Were your lips pressed tightly together and your eyebrows lowered, or was your mouth hanging open and your head tilted to one side?

Each set of nonverbals sends a different message. Those behaviors displaying concentration and involvement might have reinforced the original message to sound more like, "I am busy reading, don't bother me. I mean it, this is interesting stuff." Those behaviors displaying wandering attention and boredom might have weakened the original message so that it would sound more like, "I am busy reading, don't bother me. But if you do bother me, I won't be upset. In fact, I might even like being interrupted."

The fact that we are continually communicating is an important concept because it means that others have uninterrupted access to the responses we make to our experiences. You can't turn yourself off. This is particularly true regarding your emotional responses, for the content of nonverbal communication largely consists of feeling statements.

DIFFER and Nonverbal Messages

The Description-Interpretation-Feeling-Forgiving-Effect-Result format presented in chapter 1 provides parents with a biblically based alternative communication style. DIFFER enables you to formulate effective spoken statements. Maximum impact, however, requires that you use nonverbal communication to repeat and accent DIFFER messages.

Repeating and Accenting Messages

Repeating   By using nonverbals, it is possible to send the same message twice. Suppose Linda has had enough of Keri's talking back. After making Description, Interpretation, and Effect statements, she ends with this Result statement, spoken while pointing up the stairs:

"Since you talked back, go to your room." Linda's pointing gesture repeats the directive, "Go to your room."

Accenting   Nonverbal messages can also highlight or underscore verbal messages. For example, should Eric wish to Describe to Jimmy how he pushed his sister, he might give him a push while saying, "You pushed your sister on the stairs."

Several categories of nonverbal messages enable you to repeat and accent your DIFFER statements.

Illustrators. Parents rely on gestures to dramatize their messages. Gestures accent verbal messages by elaborating, emphasizing, and clarifying difficult and abstract concepts. Eric had little success merely telling Jimmy he was going to get a spanking the next time he defied a direct order (Result statement). However, Eric discovered that he got good compliance when he illustrated a swat on the behind by loudly clapping his hands as he said the word *spanking.*

Affect displays. Parents employ several forms of nonverbal communication to reveal their emotions. Facial expressions, posture, and vocalizations accent Feeling statements. Merely telling Keri, "I am furious," hardly disturbs her. However, saying it with a stern face—narrowed eyes and a turned-down mouth—enhances the message. A stiffened posture with the head held erect and slightly forward also intensifies the message. Finally, amplifying your feelings using various vocal qualities produces a high-impact message. Figure 1 illustrates how you can use various vocal characteristics to communicate your feelings to your children.

Figure 1
Communicating Feelings Using
Three Qualities of Vocal Expression[13]

Feeling	Loudness	Pitch	Rate
Affection	Soft	Low	Slow
Anger	Loud	High	Fast
Boredom	Moderate to low	Moderate to low	Moderately slow
Cheerful- ness	Moderately high	Moderately high	Moderately fast
Impatience	Normal	Normal to moderately high	Moderately fast
Joy	Loud	High	Fast
Sadness	Soft	Low	Slow
Satisfaction	Normal	Normal	Normal

Adaptors. Parents use a variety of nonverbal communication formats to make their children feel comfortable. Touch, eye contact, and body orientation can reduce the anxiety children feel when parents speak *Forgiving* statements. A pat, a hug, or touching your child on the shoulder can be reassuring as you forgive him.

The reassurance of touching intensifies and repeats your words of forgiveness. Face-to-face interaction with direct eye contact also intensifies and repeats the message.[14]

When we use words, we engage in linguistic behavior. However, competence in talking with your children goes beyond acquiring the ability to use words. Competence depends heavily on acquiring nonverbal skills as well. When we use nonverbals, we engage in a wide range of behaviors: body orientation, posture, gesture, facial expression, vocal variation, touch, and use of space. Effective parent-child communication requires an understanding of how verbal and nonverbal communication interconnect to produce messages. We now turn to an analysis of effective communication as a total system.

3
Being a Parent Who Understands the Communication Process

Every prudent man acts out of knowledge, but a fool exposes his folly.

Proverbs 13:16 NIV

When We Communicate

We know it isn't easy to reflect on the communication process; what you need are easily learned tips that will enable you to better relate to your children. That's why we have tried to share so many practical ideas in chapters 1 and 2. But communication is complex. Without getting too theoretical, we offer you the following short course in the subject. We encourage you to take a few minutes and carefully look at what happens when you talk with your children.

We view the communication process as a seven-piece puzzle.[1] We have laid out these seven puzzle pieces in Figure 2. Put the pieces together, and you'll have the picture.

Looking only at the scattered puzzle pieces, you might feel a bit confused at first. But once you pick out the corner pieces, you can begin putting together the puzzle. The bottom two corner pieces—PARENT and CHILD—both send and receive messages (*see* Figure 3).

As you know, the messages parents and children send take one of two forms: verbal (V) and nonverbal (NV).

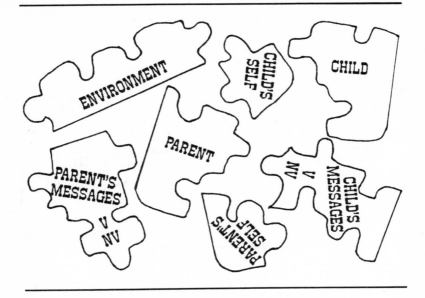

Figure 2
The Communication Puzzle

Verbal messages use words to convey what we think and feel. Nonverbal messages use behaviors to convey mostly what we feel. Figure 4 shows how verbal and nonverbal messages connect parents and children.

The content of our verbal and nonverbal messages is largely a product of our total personality. The top two corner puzzle pieces—PARENT'S SELF and CHILD'S SELF—represent the total personalities of the two communication participants (*see* Figure 5).

Who and what we are (Self) largely stems from two elements of personality: experiences and expectations. We use our known life history (past events we remember) and our unknown life history (past events we have forgotten) to form a framework for understanding the present. We access this framework by using a checklist of questions:

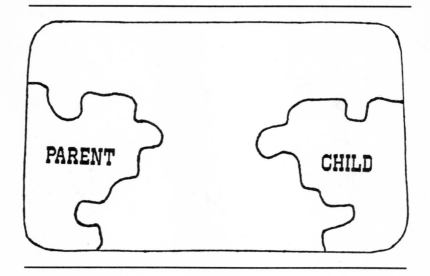

Figure 3
Parents and Children in the Communication Puzzle

"Is this a repeated experience?" "If so, what was the last outcome?" "Did I judge the last outcome good or bad?" Our answers to these questions determine the meaning we assign to the events in our lives and, ultimately, the responses we make to our experience.

In chapter 2, the conversation in which Keri complains to her mother that she never gets to go to the tape store illustrates the relationship between our meaning system and our previous experiences. Take the term *videotape,* for example. Linda and Keri both associate the word *videotape* with the object itself—a little black cartridge that holds magnetic tape. Linda knows what Keri wants. But meaning goes beyond the object itself. Meaning includes our experience with the object as well. Hearing the word *videotape,* Linda runs through her checklist: "Is this a repeated experience?" Yes, Keri has had videotapes be-

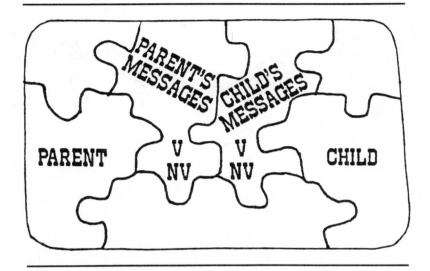

Figure 4
Verbal and Nonverbal Messages in the
Communication Puzzle

fore. "What was the last outcome?" She watched them over and over for hours on end. "Did I judge the last outcome good or bad?" Bad. Keri, on the other hand, runs through her checklist: "Is this a repeated experience?" Yes, I've had videotapes before. "What was the last outcome?" I watched them over and over for hours. "Did I judge the last outcome good or bad?" Good.

In addition to showing Linda and Keri exchanging "I want" messages, Figure 4 shows Linda and Keri simultaneously engaging in self-talk. Linda says to her (Self), "Keri wants one of those time-wasting videotapes. Those things are bubble gum for the mind." Keri says to her (Self), "I want one of those fantastic videotapes. Those things are better than candy." Unwilling or unable to share their self-talk, Keri and Linda do not disclose their

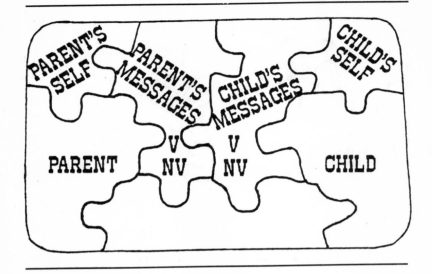

Figure 5
Total Personalities in the Communication Puzzle

widely different perceptions of videotapes. Each of them
leaves the exchange confused and a little hurt.

An unsuccessful attempt to treat a rash under Jimmy's
lower lip also illustrates how our previous experience
plays a major role in shaping our meaning system. When
Jim was four, our pediatrician prescribed the compound
benzoin tincture for his lip. It smelled like coconuts and
tropical fruits and appeared harmless. But when Eric
applied the compound, Jim screamed in agony. Only the
miraculous, curative effects of a Band-Aid could calm
him.

That afternoon, Eric decided to try to put some hydrocor-
tisone—a mild lotion—on Jim's lip. Jim ran through his
checklist: "Is this a repeated experience?" You betcha!
"What was the last outcome?" Intense pain! "Did I judge
the last outcome good or bad?" Bad. So bad that ten men

could not have held our four-year-old long enough for Eric to apply the new medication. All Jim knew was that something like this had happened before, and it stung like blazes. Realizing what lotion on the lip meant to Jim, Eric backed off. Talking would not make Jim cooperate. His body would have to heal itself.

The expectations we hold for ourselves and others form a second framework from which we operate to understand the here and now. We access this framework by using another checklist of questions: "What do I want out of this situation?" "What behaviors must I enact to get what I want?" "What behaviors must the other person(s) enact in order for me to get what I want?" Our answers to these questions determine the responses we are likely to make.

The close connection between our expectations and the responses we make to our children is also illustrated by Keri complaining to Linda that she never gets to go to the tape store. After hearing Keri express her disappointment, Linda runs through her checklist: "What do I want out of this situation?" Well, I want Keri to understand that I am a good mother, a mother who sets useful limitations for her children and enforces them. "What behaviors must I enact to get what I want?" I have to sound like a mother who knows her job and means business. "What behaviors must the other person (Keri) enact in order for me to get what I want?" Keri must think beyond her own need for self-gratification and realize that she needs external guidance and control.

Understand that Keri doesn't hear this self-talk, so when Linda tells Keri she wants her to play outside instead of watching television, Keri incorrectly interprets Linda's motivation. Keri responds as if Linda intentionally had sought to act mean and nasty. Their communication results in confusion and hurt instead of mutual understanding and acceptance.

Our expectations are so numerous that an exhaustive list would be difficult to construct. We require Keri and Jimmy to follow certain social conventions, such as saying "please" and "thank you." We insist that Keri and Jimmy extend common courtesies to us, such as phoning when they are going to be late and helping us when we are in a hurry. We expect our children to defer to our higher status, respect our authority, and obey our directives. We expect ourselves to be respectful of Keri's and Jimmy's self-concepts and to affirm each as an important person. These are the expectations known to us. We can list them when asked. But some of our expectations remain below the surface of conscious awareness, yet they influence the content of our messages.

Using the expectations that authority figures—parents, teachers, pastors—had for us, we form both our known and unknown expectations for others. We assimilate the expectations of others and later evoke them in similar situations. For example, we have a rule in our house that when the kids want to use something that belongs to Eric or Linda, they have to ask nicely; they have to say, "May I use your tape recorder, please?" Because Keri is the oldest, she was the first to assimilate the expectation implicit in this rule. Within a few days, Keri was requiring that Jim, then three years old, say the magic words *may I please* every time he touched something belonging to her. Jim, of course, reciprocated: Both kids drove each other nuts evoking their newly acquired expectation.

Each of us consults our total personality (Self) to understand the here and now. Because these consultations take the form of self-talk, our children have no way of knowing our perceptions of the here and now. Similarly, as a child consults his total personality, a parent has no way of knowing what is presently going on. An important key to successful communication is disclosing at least a portion of this self-talk and negotiating the meanings and expectations from which we will operate.

Each communication act takes place in a specific cultural, political, and technological context. The final piece to the communication puzzle, ENVIRONMENT, underscores the need for parents to consider the conditions that complicate communication with children (*see* Figure 6).

Think of the communication that occurs in the environment in which you spend most of your time—your home. Family life can be wild and crazy. At our house, we have a "Welcome" sign just inside the front door. The sign speaks of our hospitality and genuine desire to honor our

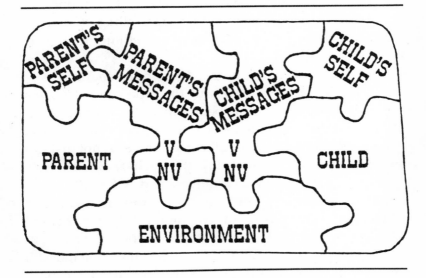

Figure 6
Environment in the Communication Puzzle

guests, but it doesn't tell the whole truth. Really, the sign should read, "Welcome to the Zoo!"

When Keri and Jimmy came to live with us, we experienced high anxiety for the first time in our lives. To help us better cope with the stress and strain, we invented the "Banana of the Day" award. This award was given to the person who, when operating under pressure, made the most laughable mistake of the day. Eric won, for example, when he had to drive home fifteen miles from work after forgetting not only his sack lunch but his briefcase, as well. Eric was also the big winner when, while at work, he noticed that his jockey shorts were on backwards! Living with two professional chaos agents can be stressful.

Three- and four-year-olds are continually on the move. They want your undivided attention, regardless of what you are doing—grabbing for a pot about to boil over on the stove, talking to your boss on the phone, or attempting to rescue their sibling from falling off a chair. It doesn't matter! When they want something, they want it NOW!

You can bet the environment affected the course of Keri and Linda's conversation about the tape store. Had Jim not been pounding on his bedroom wall with one of his blocks and the oven timer not gone off, Linda might have communicated differently. Likewise, had Keri not just lost an argument over whose toy the Etch A Sketch was, perhaps she would have communicated differently.

Parents, however, can compensate for the bedlam in which they are trying to communicate. One helpful principle is the "thirty-second rule." If you can't say it in thirty seconds, forget it. Kids aren't going to stand still for more than thirty seconds, much less listen for more than thirty seconds. The trick is to realize you can't communicate with your kids the way you communicate with your colleagues at work or with friends in the neighborhood. In fact, given the muddle and jumble in which you are likely to be operating, it is unlikely you can even talk to your spouse as you talk to others away from home. Following the thirty-second rule is one way to compensate for environmental effects associated with raising small children.

Putting It All Together

Our communication puzzle permits us to closely examine parent-child communication. The picture formed by the seven puzzle pieces shows that parent-child communication is the process by which parents and children establish and maintain primary relationships through enactment of verbal and nonverbal behavior. Our depiction suggests six characteristics of parent-child communication.

1. *Parent-child communication is a process.* Parent-child communication is not a thing. At its most basic level it consists of seven components: Parent, Child, Parent's Verbal and Nonverbal Messages, Child's Verbal and Nonverbal Messages, Parent's Self, Child's Self, and the Environment.

2. *Parent-child communication happens simultaneously.* We can't take turns communicating in a family. Both parent and child shown in Figure 6 are emitting messages at the same time. Both need not be talking during a given moment for this to occur. While the child is talking, the parent is sending nonverbal messages which the child probably is taking in and using to modify his message. The parent is working elsewhere in the communication process.

In addition to giving off a nonverbal message, the parent is busy at the same moment listening to the child's verbal message, attending to the child's nonverbal message, attending to his own nonverbal message, formulating his own verbal message by accessing his meaning system and expectations (depicted by the word Self in Figure 6), and attending to the environment in which all this is taking place.

Likewise, in addition to sending verbal and nonverbal messages simultaneous with the parent's actions, the child is attending to the verbal and nonverbal messages he is sending, formulating his next verbal and nonverbal messages by accessing his meaning system and expectations (depicted by the word Self in Figure 6), and attending to the environment in which he is communicating. It all happens at once, in the smallest unit of time—the blink of an eye.

3. *Parent-child communication is complex.* In addition to so much happening in any given moment, communication is a complex process because it is closely tied to the complexity of human beings. If everyone had identical meaning systems and identical sets of expectations, things would be a lot simpler. But there are as many different meaning systems and sets of expectations as there are people. Each time you encounter another family member, it's a new ball game. A hard and angry stare directed to Keri brings looks of confusion and sometimes tears. The same stare directed toward Jim results in looks of defiance and sometimes aggressive behavior. Each child references his or her personal history and the system of meaning that has resulted from life experiences in order to determine the meaning of our angry stares. Keri assigns one meaning to Eric's or Linda's angry stares and Jimmy assigns another. Communication is complex because it involves the total personality.

4. *Parent-child communication is irreversible.* Our communication puzzle doesn't explicitly make this point, but it strongly implies it. Because messages are noted, recorded as part of our personal history, and assigned meaning, they can't be taken back. Once emitted, our verbal and nonverbal messages can't be erased, nor can their effects be undone. This has obvious implications when harsh or unkind words are used. But beyond this implication is a more fundamental and far-reaching application.

Parents should continually monitor their behavior. When you are tired, it is so easy to emit negative and rejecting messages to your children. When you are in a hurry, the same damaging messages can occur. Amazingly, these unintended behaviors can send multiple messages. They can say to the child, "Go away, and don't come back until bedtime," and they can say parenthetically, "Don't ever remind me that I told you to go away and don't bother me." Once emitted, such uncaring messages take their place in the child's personal history. Repeated often enough, the child assigns meanings to them which the parents never intended. And there is no recalling them.

5. *Parent-child communication is dynamic.* In addition to so many things going on in the communication process, many of the seemingly endless number of variables are in a continuous state of change. Participants change. Sometimes Linda communicates with Keri alone; sometimes she communicates with Keri and Jimmy. The personal histories of parents and children change from moment to moment, not to mention from month to month and year to year. Changes in meaning systems and expectations accompany changes in personal histories. The environment shifts continually, presenting new circumstances. Since all seven communication puzzle pieces constitute a process,

changes in one puzzle piece affect the six other puzzle pieces.

6. *Parent-child communication determines our view of the world and ourselves.* Our communication puzzle underscores the role of the each participant's total personality in formulating messages to be sent and in assigning meaning to the messages received. Our communication puzzle also suggests the other side of the coin. Each communication received becomes a part of our personal history. Placing message upon message, we build our world view. Relying on this continually revised cognitive map, we make our way in the world. We come to regard the world as hostile or safe by the messages we receive. We form our self-concepts and make decisive judgments about our abilities through using the messages we get. We learn how to love or how to hate through the messages that come our way.[2]

PART II
TALKING WITH YOUR CHILDREN

The five chapters that form the second half of this book apply the principles of effective communication that help establish and maintain healthy and satisfying parent-child relationships.

Chapter 4, "Exercising Discipline," offers specific suggestions for managing behavior using DIFFER messages. Here you will find useful ideas for responding to defiance and rebellion, temper tantrums, whining, lying, and forgetting behavior.

Chapter 5, "Establishing and Maintaining Intimacy," focuses on the skillful application of active listening skills and demonstrates how to use active listening to establish intimacy between you and your child.

Chapter 6, "Building Self-Esteem," looks at how children's self-esteem is affected by the way parents address them. The chapter supplements DIFFER with a second set of message formats, the Gibb categories.

Chapter 7, "Forming Values and Acquiring Life Skills," illustrates the application of DIFFER messages to talk with children about their sexuality, peer pressure, the search for identity, drawing away from the family, love and marriage, choosing a career, how to handle money, and leaving home.

Chapter 8, "Managing Friendship," applies DIFFER messages to resolving conflict between adult children and their parents. The chapter also illustrates how to apply DIFFER messages to handle "difficult" adult children.

4
Exercising Discipline

> He who spares the rod hates his son, but he who
> loves him is careful to discipline him.
>
> Proverbs 13:24 NIV

Giving Your Child the Gift of Discipline

How's this for a one-sentence philosophy: "Life's tough,
then you die." Life is difficult. Unfortunately, many strug-
gling adults never accept this truth. They moan about their
troubles as if they had somehow been singled out for af-
fliction. But as Christians, we know everyone suffers.

> To Adam he said, "Because you listened to your
> wife and ate from the tree about which I commanded
> you, 'You must not eat of it,'
>
> "Cursed is the ground because of you; through
>   painful toil you will eat of it
>   all the days of your life.
> It will produce thorns and thistles for you,
>   and you will eat the plants of the field.
> By the sweat of your brow
>   you will eat your food
> until you return to the ground,
>   since from it you were taken;
> for dust you are and
>   to dust you will return."
>
> Genesis 3:17–19 NIV

Life is hard, and not only is that the way it is but also the
way it's supposed to be. Yet a whole generation appears
not to have gotten the message. As Christian parents, we
have an obligation to teach this truth to our children. We

need to teach them acceptance of life's problems and how to solve them.

We are teaching when we discipline children. Disciplined children become disciplined adults. Undisciplined children lack the tools to solve problems. Disciplined children can subjugate the will, delay gratification, exercise patience, assume responsibility, orient themselves to reality, accept challenge, be truthful in relationships, and lead balanced lives. Lacking these character traits, children grow up to be ineffective adults.

We discipline so children can grow in character. Disciplining to gain control over children is disciplining to increase power. Disciplining to break a child's will is disciplining to break his spirit. Disciplining to subdue the active and noisy nature of children is disciplining to convenience ourselves. Appropriate discipline always serves the child before it serves the parent. It is a gift. Once given, it can never be taken away, for with appropriate discipline, the child learns the skills he needs to accept and solve life's problems.

Rewards and Punishment, Encouragement and Consequences, and Permissiveness Too

"There is a time for everything, and a season for every activity under heaven" (Ecclesiastes 3:1 NIV).

There is no single effective disciplinary approach. Parents have three distinctly different approaches from which to choose. First, parents can opt to have authority over their children. Authoritarian parents send messages such as, "I know what's best for you. There is nothing you can tell me that I need to know to make the right decisions for you." Indeed, common sense tells us we are far better prepared than our children to know what is best for them.

We know the dangers the world presents and we can save our children a lot of trouble by making all their decisions for them. The messages sent by authoritarian parents are grounded in reality.

Second, parents can opt for a disciplinary approach that confronts their children with the consequences of reality. Reality-oriented parents send messages such as, "You learn by making your own decisions and experiencing the natural and/or logical consequences of those decisions. My job is to provide opportunities for you to make decisions and to hold you accountable for your decisions." Common sense tells us if our children are to grow and mature, they have to make their own decisions and be held accountable for those decisions. After all, the child eventually has to live his own life. The messages sent by reality-oriented parents are anchored in reality too.

Third, parents can opt for a permissive approach. Permissive parents send messages such as "You can only grow if you are free to experience life as it is." There is validity to permissiveness as well, for common sense tells us that at some point, children must operate independently of their parents. Parents can't always be there to define their children's choices. Parents can't always be there to hold their children accountable to natural consequences or to administer logical consequences. The messages sent by the permissive approach also are founded in reality.

Parents can legitimately use each of these three approaches to discipline; however, successful parents avoid bouncing back and forth between them—authoritarian rule one day followed by permissiveness the next. Skilled parents select a discipline approach appropriate to the level of a child's maturity and ability. As children develop and grow, effective parents adjust their approach to discipline.

Holding Your Child Accountable

The need to adjust your approach to the method of discipline you employ stems from three elements of reality: (1) since children have little ability and very little experience when they are young and immature, parents do know what is best for them; (2) since children acquire life skills by experiencing natural and logical consequences of their actions, children can grow and mature only when their parents hold them accountable for their behavior; and (3) since children must leave their parents and make their own way in the world, parents at some point must release their children. These three realities form the foundation for the disciplinary cycle presented in Figure 7.[1]

Two factors define each of the quadrants shown in Figure 7. These factors are level of chronological age/maturity and level of experience/ability. The age range and the range of abilities characteristic of each quadrant are as follows:

Quadrant 1.   Children in Quadrant 1 typically are younger than seven years of age. At best, they are able to pick up their toys and blocks, follow simple directions, and help with household chores.

Quadrant 2.   Children in Quadrant 2 are generally between seven and twelve years old. Probably they are able to do regular household chores, play in the neighborhood without supervision, do homework without being told to, and perhaps baby-sit the younger children in the family.

Quadrant 3.   Children in Quadrant 3 range in age from thirteen to nineteen years old. They are capable of a wide

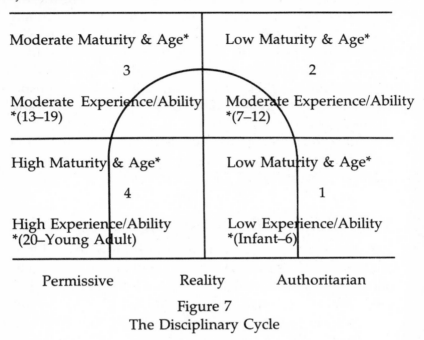

Moderate Maturity & Age* 3 Moderate Experience/Ability *(13–19)	Low Maturity & Age* 2 Moderate Experience/Ability *(7–12)
High Maturity & Age* 4 High Experience/Ability *(20–Young Adult)	Low Maturity & Age* 1 Low Experience/Ability *(Infant–6)

Permissive   Reality   Authoritarian

Figure 7
The Disciplinary Cycle

range of independence. They may hold part-time jobs, date regularly, and drive a car.

Quadrant 4.   Children in Quadrant 4 are really young adults ranging upward from twenty years of age. They are likely to be separating from parental responsibility, setting their own hours, spending money as they see fit, owning their own cars, and freely deciding if they are to attend church.[2]

Figure 7 also presents three disciplinary approaches arranged on a continuum of parental involvement and action. At the left end of the continuum is authoritarian discipline. Authoritarian parents tend to use corporal

punishment—spanking their children for serious rule in-
fractions or challenges to their authority. "Spare the rod
and spoil the child." This misquoted Bible verse actually
reads: "He who spares the rod hates his son, but he who
loves him is careful to discipline him" (Proverbs 13:24
NIV).[3] In biblical times, shepherds used rods (short, thick
clubs) to protect their flocks from wolves. It is probable
that shepherds also used their rods to punish unruly and
defiant children.

Could their harsh methods of discipline have application
today? After all, these were simple and unenlightened
men. Haven't we come a long way since then?

Why Children Enact Unacceptable Behavior

Psychologist Kevin Leman declares his love for children
but then observes that his love for them doesn't make him
blind to reality. That's why he affectionately says, "Children are the enemy!"[4] The reality which Dr. Leman
recognizes is that children often seek to get their own way
and frequently act out of selfishness. Acting as such,
children interfere with the needs of parents.

Why don't children instinctively take others into account, avoiding what appears to be senseless conflict?
Why is rebellion standard equipment in every child who
rolls off the production line? What makes children univer-
sally willfully defiant?

Few textbooks on child development and behavior
address this side of children. Most authors prefer to
address the roots of childish irresponsibility: Why Johnny
forgets to feed the dog, or make his bed, or brush his
teeth. Pick up just about any book on raising children and
you'll get good advice on how to help your child assume
responsibility. But most books offer little insight into why

children disobey. Why is it that when you ask your child to stop playing with the buttons on the microwave, he looks at you and his eyes say, "I know what you want, but I am not going to do it, and I want to know what you are going to do about it."

Is this inborn sin?

> The Lord God took the man and put him in the Garden of Eden to work it and take care of it. And the Lord God commanded the man, "You are free to eat from any tree in the garden; but you must not eat from the tree of knowledge of good and evil, for when you eat of it you will surely die."
>
> Genesis 2:15–17 NIV

> When the woman saw that the fruit of the tree was good for food and pleasing to the eye, and also desirable for gaining wisdom, she took some and ate it. She also gave some to her husband, who was with her, and he ate it.
>
> Genesis 3:6 NIV

Mommy puts four-year-old Johnny in the kitchen and tells him, "You can play with the buttons on the dish washer, the knobs on the radio [which she unplugs], and the knobs on the cabinets, but don't play with the buttons on the microwave; if you do I will spank you." When Johnny sees that buttons and knobs are fun to play with, he looks at the microwave buttons, reaches up, and begins to play with them. Then he lets his three-year-old sister play with them. The parallelism is hard to ignore.

The Disciplinary Cycle

As parents, our job is to enable our children to come to terms with their rebellious nature and to discipline them-

selves to function within the boundaries of their power in
a cooperative relationship with society. We begin this
process by exercising authoritarian discipline.

Authoritarian Discipline

Quadrant 1 in Figure 7 identifies when authoritarian discipline is appropriate. During early childhood,
when an individual is both immature and inexperienced, authoritarian discipline lets the child know he is a
separate entity in the world with limited power over
that world. Through authoritarian discipline, the child
learns that his wish is not his parents' command. The
child learns to restrict his ego, setting appropriate boundaries within which his ego can operate. Authoritarian
discipline communicates to the child an important reality:
His parents have rules and the fortitude to enforce their
rules. During this period in Keri's and Jimmy's
development, we followed the advice of an old and
trusted friend: "If they need a spanking, give 'em a
spanking."

Dr. Kevin Leman has set forth a number of useful
guidelines for spanking children (enumeration ours):

1. Children under eighteen months should never
    be swatted.
2. A swat on the bottom can be a very good
    disciplinary measure for a young child in the
    two- to seven-year-old range when he is being
    absolutely willful and rebellious.
3. The key to spanking a child is being in control of
    your own emotions. While it seems a contradic-
    tion, spanking is something that must be done in
    love. True, you may not feel very loving while
    administering the spanking, but the way you
    show your love is by not losing your cool.

4. Some child-rearing specialists advise never to swat a child with your hand. They say to use a ruler or a paddle. I disagree with that approach. The same hand that guides a child across a busy street must sometimes discipline to help him learn.

5. I believe that when you spank a child, you have an obligation to tell the child exactly why he was spanked. Hold the child and talk to him about your feelings. Explain what made you angry and why it was necessary to spank. Explain what you expect from the child in the future.[5]

Managing Defiance and Rebellion   We use DIFFER, the format for parental communication presented in chapter 1, to structure our follow-up talks. Use of DIFFER puts the spankings we give our children into focus. The DIFFER format enables us to say to our children, "I reject your behavior, but I accept you." Its healing effect promotes intimacy and affection between us.

Jimmy: Whaa-whaa!

Eric: When you're quiet, we'll talk, Jimmy.

Jimmy: (*quiet now*)

Eric: Jimmy, I asked you three times to stop hitting the coffee table with your blocks, but you didn't stop [description statement]. I am wondering if you don't think I mean what I say [interpretation statement]. I am tired of your ignoring me when I tell you to stop [feeling statement].

Jimmy: (*nods his head while drying his tears*)

Eric: Jimmy, Daddy's job is to care for you and look out for you, but when you disobey me, I can't do my job [effect statement]. I want you to know that no one, including you, is going to keep me from doing my job. Are you with me, son? What's my job?

Jimmy: To take care of me.

Eric: That's right. Now I want you to know I hope I don't have to spank you again this morning, but if you disobey me again, I will spank you again [result statement].

Jimmy: Okay.

Eric: I love you, son. There's nothing you can do or say that will make me stop loving you [feeling statement]. I forgive you for hitting the coffee table with your blocks when I told you to stop [forgiving statement]. I know you can listen to me and do what I ask you to do. Okay, let's go see what Keri is doing.

Managing Temper Tantrums and Whining Behavior

In addition to the defiance and rebellion characteristic of Quadrant 1, parents frequently face a second category of problem behavior enacted by young and inexperienced children: temper tantrums. Defiance and temper tantrums share the same objective: control of parents. However, unlike defiance, which is a form of direct resistance, temper tantrums are a form of passive resistance.

Let's face it—kids take power trips to test their parents' resolve and stamina. When parents effectively extinguish the direct resistance manifested by defiant behavior, children often change to the alternative strategy of indirect resistance, which they enact in the form of temper tantrums or whining and fussing. Although maladaptive, such behavior has a definite purpose: to keep parents involved in the child's life. Kids want to know who's in charge, and when they can't exercise defiance, they are not above temper tantrums. In addition, children want attention, and they often can get it by whining and fussing.

Since temper tantrums and their close cousins, whining and fussing, are acts of indirect resistance, parents should employ an alternative strategy developed by psychologist

Kevin Leman: reality discipline.[6] Reality discipline is neither authoritarian nor permissive. Suppose your child
runs into the street and he is almost hit by a passing car.
Probably you would want to talk to your child about what
happened and firmly caution him against disregarding
your directives in the future, but you wouldn't want to
spank him. Why? Because the natural consequence, the
sight of that car bearing down on him, the sound of its
screeching brakes and blasting horn, would be enough
punishment. A natural consequence is one that simply
happens. Rock in your chair when you should be sitting
still, and fall off and bump your head. That's a natural
consequence.

In addition to using natural consequences, reality
discipline employs logical consequences. Logical consequences are outcomes closely connected to, but separate
from, the events of a situation. Natural consequences are
what reality *does*. Logical consequences are what reality
says. Parents usually outline logical consequences ahead
of time by telling the child what will happen if he
behaves in a certain way. This is called "setting the
contingency." Should your child run into the street and
have nothing happen to him, reality says, "Kid, you were
lucky this time, but you could have been hit by a car." If
you want to provide your child with a logical consequence for this kind of behavior, you might tell him he'll
lose out on going to the park (your original destination) if
he runs into the street.

Reality discipline is an ideal approach to temper tantrums and whining. Suppose you are shopping and your
child takes an expensive toy from the shelf and puts it in
your cart. Since you don't want him to have the toy, you
say, "You really want that toy, don't you?" He says,
"Yes." And you reply, "Well, we're not shopping for toys

today. We'll consider buying this when we go shopping for your birthday." To which he drops to the floor, kicking and shouting, "I want it! I want it!" You stand back and allow reality to happen.

The reality is that you have places to go. So you say, "You can act like that if you want to, but I am leaving." Then you head for the door. After you take those first few steps, nine times out of ten, your child will be running after you shouting, "Wait! Wait!" Why? Because his temper tantrum has failed to control you.

What should you do if your child doesn't follow you? Keep walking, but never let him out of your sight. Stop at the door or look at a few items one or two counters away. Stay out of his sight, if possible. Sooner or later, he'll discover he's lost! Unless he is an extremely difficult child, being lost should be a reality experience sufficiently traumatizing to teach him a lesson.

How about that whining and fussing that grates on so many parents? Do you just walk away from that too? Sure. Walking away is a nonverbal message that says, "I don't want to be around you when you whine and fuss." Walking away is letting reality happen. Of course, sometimes you won't want to leave the room. Perhaps leaving the room means leaving your favorite chair. Or maybe you've laid out your work, and moving all those papers would be inconvenient. What then? Time for administering a logical consequence. Take your child firmly by the arm, walk him to his room, and as you put him in his room say, "If you want to act like that, you can whine and fuss in your room. When you're quiet, we'll talk." Close the door and go back to what you were doing.

When your child is quiet, open the door, sit him on a chair, and establish eye contact. Although the reality of your logical consequence has already taught him a valuable lesson, a follow-up talk using the DIFFER format can be both reinforcing and comforting. Such a follow-up talk might sound like this:

Linda: When I told you no, you couldn't have a snack, you said, "Noooooooo! I waaaaaaaaant aaaaaaaah snaaaaaaaaaak." You said that while you shook your arms and stamped your feet. That's whiny and fussy behavior [description statement]. I am beginning to think you believe you can get what you want by making things unpleasant for me [interpretation statement].

Keri: I'm sorry.

Linda: I accept your apology and I forgive you [forgiving statement], but I want you to know that I get annoyed when you act whiny and fussy [feeling statement]. When you annoy me, I don't want to be around you [effect statement]. The next time you act whiny and fussy, I am going to put you in your room again [result statement]. What am I going to do if you're fussy and whiny again?

Keri: Put me in my room.

Linda: Right. Now I know you can cooperate and accept my decisions. Let's try to be more respectful of each other.

Quadrant 1 in Figure 7 depicts the use of an authoritarian approach to manage defiance and rebellion, followed by an increasing use of reality discipline to manage temper tantrums and the related forms of passive resistance, whining and fussing. The evolution from authoritarian discipline to reality discipline should be complete by as early as age seven and no later than age twelve.

Reality Discipline

Quadrant 2 in Figure 7 depicts a heavy reliance on reality discipline to manage two new behavior problems: talking back and lying. Since success in managing the behaviors characteristic of Quadrant 2 is heavily dependent on skillful application of reality discipline, we'll take a moment to outline a number of basic principles:

Reality Discipline Tutorial

---

1. *Allow reality to happen.* In situations where the child's health and welfare will not be endangered by experiencing natural consequences, let the child suffer the consequences of his actions. To paraphrase a well-known Bible verse, "As a man reaps what he sows, so should a child" (Galatians 6:7).

2. *Replace natural consequences with logical consequences.* In situations where the child's health and welfare are endangered by natural consequences, impose logical consequences. Similarly, in situations where the negative effects of natural consequences are suppressed by social convention or too separated in time from the child's behavior, impose logical consequences.

3. *Set the contingency.* When using logical consequences, tell your child ahead of time the action you intend to take if he enacts certain behavior.

4. *Use logical consequences that are truly logical.* Be sure the contingencies you set are closely tied to your child's negative behavior.

5. *Use logical consequences that train and teach.* Logical consequences that merely punish are inappropriate.

6. *Take immediate and direct action.* Be sure the logical consequences you impose closely follow your child's wrongful behavior.

7. *Point out reality as the source of suffering caused by logical consequences.* Show your child that you are not causing the pain he feels—reality is.

Managing Sassy and Disrespectful Behavior   Using the DIFFER format and the basic principles of reality discipline, parents can effectively manage the two behavior problems characteristic of Quadrant 2: talking back and lying. Sassy and disrespectful replies to your directives are

really acts of rebellion and defiance. If the authority issue
was never resolved in Quadrant 1, then your child's
talking back is merely a continuation of his challenge to
your leadership. If, on the other hand, the authority issue
was resolved back in Quadrant 1, then your child is
regressing. Such regression is perfectly normal and hardly
cause for alarm. Your child is saying, in effect, "Okay, you
wouldn't stand for my defiant no's, but I am bigger now
and maybe you'll crack if I tell you to buzz off." If ever
there was an issue you wanted to win and win big, this is
it. Through exercising the DIFFER format and reality
discipline, you can set your child straight regarding your
authority. Here's how:

Eric: Jimmy, put your shoes on before you go outside.

Jimmy: I don't want to wear my shoes.

Eric: (*taking Jimmy by the shoulders*) Put your shoes on.

Jimmy: You're stupid and yucky.

Eric: (*sitting Jimmy on a chair*) You just called me stupid
and yucky [description statement]. I am wondering if
you're interested in how much abuse and disrespect I'll
take from you [interpretation statement].

Jimmy: I'm sorry.

Eric: Maybe you were just mad at me [interpretation
statement].

Jimmy: Ya.

Eric: I want you to know it's okay to be angry with me,
but when you express your anger with sassy talk I feel
hurt and angry [feeling statement]. When you talk back to
me, it undermines our relationship [effect statement]. It's
hard for me to look out for you and take care of you when
you are disrespectful of the authority I have because I am
your father [effect statement].

Jimmy: I don't want to wear my shoes.

Eric: I understand that you don't want to wear your
shoes. But because it's cold outside, I decided that you

need shoes to keep your feet warm. Now, if you don't like my decision, it's okay to be angry with me for making you wear your shoes. You can say, "I get mad when I am told what to wear." But it's not okay to say sassy words like *stupid* and *yucky*.

Jimmy: Okay.

Eric: One more thing, son. The next time you sass me, it's going to cost you something. You want to go outside, don't you? Well, if you're sassy again, I am not going to feel much like letting you go outside [result statement]. Are you with me, son?

Jimmy: Ya.

Eric: Okay, I forgive you for calling me names [forgiving statement]. I know you can talk to me in a respectful manner. Now go put your shoes on and you can play outside.

When responding to your child's "smart mouth," it is important not to feed back a similar message such as, "Listen, you little brat, you can't talk to me like that." If your child becomes disrespectful, you shouldn't become disrespectful in return. If the child is to learn respect for others, he needs to be treated with respect. That's why parents need to keep their tempers under control. If necessary, leave the room for a few minutes before returning to deliver a response that follows the principles illustrated in the above example.

Whatever you do, insist that your children treat you with respect. Never accept sassy behavior. Furthermore, mothers should never allow their sons to verbally abuse them and fathers should never take any smart mouth from their daughters. The relationship between mothers and sons and fathers and daughters is very powerful. When parents hold the line with opposite-sex children, they are increasing their children's chances for a successful marriage. By insisting on respect from their opposite-sex children, parents teach a number of important lessons about respect and love in marriage.

Managing Lying Behavior Unlike talking back, which can be traced to a single issue—rebellion—lying has a number of underlying causes. The lies of very young children often are simple fantasy or wish fulfillment. Lies are their imaginary friends and siblings, or stories about skills they don't yet possess, such as the ability to read. Even claims of having cleaned their rooms when they didn't are often just expressions of how very young children would like things to be. These lies are really harmless and can be safely ignored.

Older children who have experienced frequent and severe punishment will frequently lie out of fear. They are afraid to tell their parents of their guilt because of what will happen to them. Our hearts go out to these children. Their parents have placed them in a double bind: Either lie to avoid punishment or tell the truth and suffer a painful experience. Few experiences are more stressful.

We have sought to avoid placing our children in this situation by sharing our own imperfections with Keri and Jimmy. When we break something we admit it to the family. For example, if Eric breaks one of Linda's good cups, he says to Keri and Jimmy, "Oh, I know I should have been more careful with Mommy's cups, but I was in a hurry. When Mommy comes home, I'll be sure and tell her how this happened."

When Linda comes home, Eric waits until Keri and Jimmy are present—for example, at the table after dinner—before showing Linda the broken cup and explaining what happened. Linda then responds in a nonpunitive manner, "I sure liked that cup. I hope you'll be more careful the next time you wash them. But I know accidents happen, and I forgive you." Then when Keri or

Jimmy uses a similar approach to tell us about something they've done, we reinforce their honesty by saying, "I appreciate your telling me what happened. I know that wasn't easy to do, but being honest is always better than telling a lie." If we have to punish, we punish with restraint and respect for the offending child.

Older children also lie for a less forgivable reason: defiance and rebellion. Suppose you tell your child he is not to climb in a neighbor's tree. He knows the strategy of open rebellion he tried earlier in his life won't work, so it's unlikely he'll look you in the eye and say, "No, I want to climb that tree and I am going to climb that tree." He also knows the strategies of passive resistance—temper tantrums, whining, and fussing—are unlikely to work. Finally, he knows he can't talk back. But he really wants to climb that tree. So he lies.

Such lies require immediate and effective action. Here again, you want to win and win big. Through use of the DIFFER format and reality discipline, you can set your child straight regarding your authority. Your confrontation with your child might sound something like this:

Eric: Mrs. Douglas called to complain that you were climbing in her tree this afternoon. What can you tell me about this?

Jimmy: I wasn't climbing in her dumb tree.

Eric: Why do you think Mrs. Douglas said you were climbing in her tree?

Jimmy: I don't know. Maybe she made a mistake.

Eric: She said you were wearing blue pants, a red jacket, and a yellow hat. You're wearing blue pants, a red jacket, and a yellow hat. She didn't make a mistake, but you're telling a lie [description statement].

Jimmy: I am not lying, honest.

Eric: I am wondering if you've said to yourself, "I don't care what Dad says, I am going to climb Mrs. Douglas' tree [interpretation statement]."

Jimmy: I'm not hurting that tree. Why can't I climb it?

Eric: You know when you lie to me, I don't think you respect my authority and that makes me angry [interpretation and feeling statement].

Jimmy: Okay, I won't climb her dumb tree anymore.

Eric: How about telling me lies?

Jimmy: Okay, I won't tell you any more lies.

Eric: I'm glad to hear that because there can't be any trust between people who lie to each other, and relationships are built on trust. If I can't trust you to tell me the truth, I can't be the kind of father I want to be [effect statement].

Jimmy: Okay.

Eric: If you keep telling me lies, I can't regard you as a grown-up boy. And that means I can't let you do some of the things you've been asking me to let you do—things like taking an airplane trip to Grandpa John's house by yourself. So if you want to do the things grown-up boys do, you need to tell the truth.

Jimmy: Okay, Dad.

Eric: Okay. I forgive you for not telling me the truth [forgiving statement]. I know you can be truthful with me in the future.

Quadrant 2 in Figure 7 depicts heavy reliance on reality discipline to manage two higher forms of defiance and rebellion: talking back and lying. To deal effectively with these problem behaviors, parents can put the principles of reality discipline into effect by using the DIFFER format. In particular, result statements can be effective since they set logical consequences as contingencies. If your child continues to talk back or lie after you have discussed these problems with him using the DIFFER format, by all means take action and evoke the consequences you discussed.

Quadrant 3 in Figure 7 depicts continued reliance on reality discipline to manage two new behavior problems: cooperation and forgetting. But then notice how the curve in Quadrant 3 rapidly plunges toward a permissive approach to discipline. This rapid progression to permissiveness makes it critical that early in Quadrant 3, parents resolve problems of cooperation and forgetting and any previous unresolved behavior problems. The opportunity to exercise active discipline over your child is quickly coming to an end.

Managing Cooperation   Getting children to comply with your directives can be an uphill battle. When you issue a directive and your child responds with an outright no, whines and fusses, throws a temper tantrum, or answers back, you are facing rebellious and defiant behavior. You know how to use reality discipline to handle rebellious and defiant behavior. But when you issue a directive and your child fails to follow through either by not complying or by making only a halfhearted effort, he or she is being uncooperative. Rather than stemming from rebellion or defiance, it is more likely the uncooperative behavior stems from a child's lazy and/or manipulative nature.

Young children love to cook and clean because doing Mommy's and Daddy's work gives them a sense of increased importance in the family. Older children typical of Quadrant 3 often regard work as something to be avoided at any cost. If older children can manipulate their parents into doing their work, they will. Usually they employ a wide range of stalling techniques until the parents conclude it is easier for them to do the assigned chores than to make the children do them.

While it is indeed annoying and frustrating to endure a child's attempts at manipulation, parents should remain quiet and firm. Avoid verbal or physical abuse. Nagging your child would be equally harmful. While parents may get results using these inappropriate disciplinary techniques, they are really not teaching cooperation. Rather, parents who shout and nag are teaching their children intimidation techniques that they will later employ to gain cooperation. Again, the ideal strategy to obtain cooperation is reality discipline. Here the reality is clear: "If you don't cooperate with me, kid, I may not necessarily cooperate with you." Here's how you can get this reality across using the DIFFER format:

Linda: Keri, I told you to clean your room this morning and now it's after lunch and your room is still a mess [description statement].

Keri: Don't worry, I'll clean my room.

Linda: I am beginning to wonder if you think I am going to clean your room, if you wait long enough [interpretation statement].

Keri: I said I'll clean my room, Mom.

Linda: It's really irritating when you don't follow through on the things I tell you to do [feeling statement].

Keri: Okay, okay.

Linda: When I am irritated as I am irritated now, I don't feel like cooperating when you want something from me [effect statement].

Keri: I'm sorry, Mom. I'll clean my room right now.

Linda: I'd appreciate that. I forgive you for dragging your feet [forgiving statement], but I want you to know if I don't get cooperation for the rest of the day, I am not taking you to the park tonight [result statement].

Keri: All right.

Managing Forgetting Behavior   Use of reality discipline to manage cooperation enables parents to stay in control and teach their children to be responsible. Reality discipline is an equally effective strategy for handling the problem of forgetting. Like lack of cooperation, forgetting often is a manipulative ploy. Here the reality you want to evoke might sound something like this: "If you forget your responsibilities, you still have an obligation to do the work, even if performing a forgotten task is inconvenient." Here's how you can impress the element of reality on your child using the DIFFER format:

Eric: Did you brush your teeth, son?

Jimmy: Oh, I forgot (*half-apologetically*).

Eric: That's the third time this week you've forgotten to brush your teeth after lunch [description statement].

Jimmy: (*smiles a silly smile and tilts his head*)

Eric: I am wondering if you think if you forget something you won't have to do it [interpretation statement].

Jimmy: (*puts his head down and shuffles his feet*)

Eric: I am getting tired of having to check up on you to see if you remembered to brush your teeth [feeling statement]. When you continually forget to brush your teeth, I have to take time to remind you and you have to stop what you're doing and brush them [effect statement].

Keri: The show is starting.

Jimmy: (*runs for the stairs*)

Eric: Hold it. You have your teeth to brush [result statement].

Jimmy: The show is starting. I'll miss the beginning.

Eric: That's right. Brush your teeth [result statement].

Quadrant 3 in Figure 7 depicts continued reliance on reality discipline to manage two additional behavior problems: cooperation and forgetting. As mentioned above, Quadrant 3 represents the last opportunity for parents to use active discipline. After age nineteen and probably before then, parents lose the ability to control their children by evoking logical consequences. The young adult, now away from the home more than he is in the home, is rapidly approaching self-sufficiency.

Permissive Discipline

Quadrant 4 in Figure 7 depicts a rapid shift to permissive discipline. By our use of the term *permissive* we do not mean the type of discipline that says, "Whatever you want is fine with me. Do as you wish." Rather, our use of the word *permissive* means that parents must now "permit" reality to happen. Where in Quadrants 2 and 3 parents substituted logical consequences for natural ones to protect their children from the physical and psychological pain associated with the natural consequence of reality, in Quadrant 4 parents must step aside and let the natural consequences of their child's behavior happen. Two reasons support the need for this tough and hard-nosed approach: First, as mentioned above, parents are no longer in a position to evoke logical consequences. Lacking authority, parents are released from their responsibility to control their children. Where there is no authority, there is no responsibility. Second, coping with the natural consequences of reality is necessary for your child to develop his ability to be accountable and responsible. Parents who bail out their young adult, rescuing him from the natural consequences of his behavior, are undermining his self-confidence and weakening his ability to cope with life.

Again, let's be sure we have made ourselves perfectly clear in presenting our definition of permissive discipline. Suppose your young adult is abusing alcohol. He is drinking regularly and occasionally to excess. He's making a big mistake, and you know it. Since he is of legal drinking age, you decide to exercise permissive discipline.

Do you then say nothing? Do you tell him it's his own
business and he should do as he wishes? No, that's not
what we mean by permissive discipline. You need to
confront him with his drinking, which you regard as a
mistake. You need to outline for him the natural consequences of his behavior while making it clear that if and
when they occur, you will not intervene to spare him pain
and anguish. Using the DIFFER format, your confrontation might sound something like this:

Eric: Jim, last night you did some heavy drinking, and
that's the fifth time this month you've abused alcohol
[description statement].

Jim: I didn't know you were keeping count.

Eric: I am wondering if drinking so much is important
to your breaking away from your mother and me [inter-
pretation statement].

Jim: Hey, it's just to party down.

Eric: Apart from doing damage to your body, your
drinking could result in a drunk-driving arrest, or worse
yet, in an accident [effect statement].

Jim: Don't worry; I can handle what I drink.

Eric: Your mother and I think you are making a big
mistake, son, and we're praying that you'll realize it
before something very painful happens to you. But listen
to me. If you're arrested, it's going to be hard; your
mother and I won't help you. So before you drink heavily
again, remember—get mixed up with the law, and you are
on your own [result statement].

Jim: Okay. I'll remember that, Dad.

Letting go is so hard. We can't imagine saying anything
more difficult than, "We won't help; you're on your own."
Yet once reality has imposed its pain and the lesson has
been learned, we know, like the father of the prodigal son
of whom Jesus spoke, we can welcome our repentant
children home without accusations and embrace them

with our unconditional love. This is permissive discipline, the end of the disciplinary life cycle that permits parents to comply with their biblical mission: "Fathers, do not exasperate your children; instead, bring them up in the training and instruction of the Lord" (Ephesians 6:4 NIV).

5
Establishing and Maintaining Intimacy

Better a meal of vegetables where there is love than
a fattened calf with hatred.

Proverbs 15:17 NIV

Alienated Families

We have all seen alienated families. Their dysfunctional relationships daily undermine and erode the cornerstone of mental health: nurturing love. We have seen the hurt that negative parents and hostile children suffer. "How do they do it?" we ask. "How do they manage to hang in there, day in and day out?"

We are talking about families in which the father doesn't realize that family members have a reality apart from their immediate impact on him. We are talking about families in which the mother can't conceptualize other family members as fully functioning individuals who experience the same emotions: hope and fear, joy and sorrow, love and hate. We are talking about families in which children manipulate others as if they were mere objects. We are talking about people who can't get beyond the irritation inherent in family life; people without empathy; people who don't express warmth and affection; people who are closed and unapproachable because they have found no joy in life.

One can only wonder what events led these estranged people to adopt their negative and hostile attitudes. Probably, we could trace the roots of their alienation to their relationship with their parents. Alienated families produce alienated people. However, we are all aware of exceptions to this rule. Some of the most loving and supportive people we know were raised by angry and hostile parents, but they chose to be different. They chose to be affectionate, caring, empathic people. They worked through their alienation to become open and loving. While we can't control whether or not we are born into an alienated family, apparently we can control our responses to the alienation we experience. Where there is no joy, we can choose joy. Effective parents choose joy. Tim Hansel provides these insights into what joy is and how we can come by it:

> It [joy] is not a feeling; it is a choice. It is not based upon circumstances; it is based upon attitude. It is free, but it is not cheap. It is the by-product of a growing relationship with Jesus Christ. It is a promise, not a deal. It is available to us when we make ourselves available to him. It is something that we can receive by invitation and by choice. It requires commitment, courage, and endurance.
>
> When Paul listed the fruit of the Spirit, he named joy second, reminding us that joy is a very high priority in the Christian walk. A friend once asked if it were possible that the listing meant that joy was the second most important virtue in the Christian faith. It's worth considering. Another friend looked at the first three—love, joy, and peace—and commented, "I never realized that it was joy that holds love and peace together."
>
> I am certain that joy is far more important than any of us ever imagined. And I am certain that it is far more available than any of us has ever dreamed.[1]

The importance of joyful parents to the process of forming fully functioning, cohesive families is difficult to overstate. Joyful parents tell their children, "We love you just because you're you." Children of joyful parents know they are loved unconditionally, not because they *are* something or *can do* something. By accepting their children as they are—flawed and imperfect—joyful parents create a climate in which children can ask their questions and share their problems. Joyful parents are aware that their children think, feel, and grow continually, not just when they are in the presence of their parents. By celebrating the separate identities of their children and respecting the fact that their children largely exist and have their being independent of them, joyful parents create an environment conducive to establishing and maintaining intimacy.

The High Cost of Alienation

Teenage suicide now stands as the second leading cause of death among adolescents. Each year, a reported sixty-five thousand young people commit suicide, and five hundred thousand more attempt it.[2] Recently, a midwestern community was rocked when over a two-week period, three students from the same high school attempted suicide. Tragically, two of these attempts were successful. The headline in the local newspaper read, "Deaths of High School Students Shock Friends, Teachers." The article told the stories of a sixteen-year-old junior and a fifteen-year-old sophomore who apparently took their own lives just days apart. Several classmates said both had seemed to have problems with their parents.

Of course, we don't know why those students died, but their tragic deaths underscore the importance of columnist Norman Podhoretz' analysis of teenage problems. According to Podhoretz, two sociologists, Peter Uhlenberg and David Eggebeen of the University of North Carolina, writing in *The Public Interest,* stated that they suspect the bond between child and parent may be the most critical determinant of all in the deteriorating condition of American adolescents. Podhoretz writes:

> Focusing their attention on this "determinant," the two sociologists find hard statistical evidence for what we all know simply from looking around. They find more and more people for whom "self-fulfillment" takes precedence over all other values.
>
> Accordingly, they find fewer and fewer people who believe in sacrificing themselves, or even their own convenience, to the needs and demands of their children. Thus an astonishing two-thirds of all American parents feel that "parents should be free to live their own lives even if it means spending less time with their children."
>
> It is to this declining commitment that, they suggest, we should turn for an explanation of the horrible fact that, during a period when presumably beneficial changes were being made in all the other features of family structure, as well as in schools and government programs, "the proportion of adolescents behaving in ways destructive to themselves and others grew ever larger."[3]

Healthy Families

Taking the Time

Healthy families make time for their children. Taking time for children doesn't mean spending every spare moment together. Family psychologist John Rosemond, author of *The Six-Point Plan for Raising Happy, Healthy Children* (Andrews and McMeel, 1989), tells the following story:

Several months ago, I was talking to an audience of several hundred people, most of whom were parents of elementary-age children.

In the middle of the presentation, I asked the audience to participate in an exercise.

I began by asking, "How many of you feel that you give your children more attention than your parents gave you as a child?"

Almost everyone raised his hand, and there was general laughter.

I then asked, "Of those of you who raised your hands, how many feel that your children need more attention than you received as a child?"

About 10 people raised their hands, and again, there was general laughter.

I've repeated this exercise before nearly a dozen audiences since, always with the same results.

Very interesting, don't you agree?[4]

In her book *Retreads,* Prudence Mackintosh explodes the myth that parents of successful families spend large amounts of quality time with their children. She says:

Children are supposed to be eager for time alone with busy fathers, but how many times have I seen the dirty station wagon roll in from a fishing trip with three disgruntled, ungrateful children. "I'm mad at Dad. He made us have a snipe hunt, and I am never going fishing with him again," one growls as they drag the fishing gear to the garage. The visits to the museums, the weekend in the country, the Great American Vacation from which no one seems to remember a thing except "the souvenir shop where you wouldn't let me buy a peppermint patty" are, with few exceptions, all relegated to that vast area of childhood known as "Someday you'll be glad we did this."

> When I reflect on all my years of mothering,
> however, it's the ordinary intimacies that I still find
> the most miraculous.[5]

These "ordinary intimacies" are the dozens of contacts your child initiates with you each day. Usually, they require no more than thirty seconds to resolve. Most of the time, the contact your child initiates involves a problem he's having:

Jimmy: Keri hit me.

Linda: Getting hit hurts.

Jimmy: She hit me on my arm.

Linda: Nobody likes getting hit.

All Jimmy wanted was a little sympathy. Sure, it took a bit longer to meet his emotional needs than to say, "Don't bother me; I'm busy," but look at the intimacy built by being responsive. The second category of contacts your child initiates involve his ego needs:

Keri: Look at what I made, Daddy.

Eric: Boy, what a terrific picture.

Keri: It's a rainbow.

Eric: It is a rainbow. And look, it has six colors.

Keri just needed to show somebody what she did and receive a little praise. How long does it take to say, "Good job"? The final category of contacts your child initiates consists of his questions:

Keri: (*interrupting a conversation between Eric and Linda, who are discussing Eric's employee evaluation*) What's an evaluation?

Linda: Just a minute, Keri. Your father and I are still talking. It will be your turn to ask a question in a minute. (*Linda and Eric finish their conversation*) Okay, Keri. What was your question?

Keri: What's an evaluation?

Linda: An evaluation is what someone thinks about

something. When you draw a picture and I say, "Good
job," I am giving you my evaluation.

Keri: Oh.

Even if your child initiates fifty such contacts a day,
resolving them in thirty seconds or less means an invest-
ment of only twenty-five minutes. Taking time for your
children simply means being approachable.

Being Open

In addition to taking time for their children, the parents
of healthy families are intimate with their children. Few
parents, of course, are willing to share their real concerns,
feelings, and problems with their children. They ask,
"Won't complete self-disclosure frighten my child?" Probably. But complete self-disclosure is not needed. Parents
can share a part of what is going on in their lives. Sharing
some of our anxieties and worries makes us appear far
more human to our children. Opening ourselves makes
our children feel more comfortable opening themselves to
us. They reason, "If Mom and Dad worry, they'll understand why I am afraid and worried."

Open and disclosing parents enable their children to see
them as imperfect. From imperfect parents, children learn
to accept their own imperfection. And from Christian
parents who confess their imperfection in prayer, children
learn to seek God's grace. Praying your heartfelt thoughts
with your children is an effective way to share with them
the harsh realities of life.

By far the most effective way to break down the barriers
that separate children from parents is to apologize for
mistakes. Going to your child when you have acted
wrongly—falsely accusing him, speaking harshly to him,
or wrongly punishing him—and asking his forgiveness
underscores your imperfection. No single act so effectively

bonds children to their parents. Kevin Leman says it best in the closing paragraph of *The Birth Order Book:*

> I believe the time we really look big in a child's eyes is when we go to them to apologize for our mistakes, not theirs. I believe the words no parent can do without are *I was wrong. Will you forgive me?*[6]

Active Listening

Joyful parents take time for their children and self-disclose to them. But the quantity of time spent with children and the degree to which parents are open with them are only two factors in the total equation: Intimacy = Time spent with children (Number of Parental Self-Disclosures + Number of Child-Owned Problems Handled by Active Listening). The third factor, active listening, is a therapeutic technique developed and used by psychologist Carl R. Rogers in his clinical practice. Active listening consists of two elements: *restatement* of another's verbal messages and *rephrasing* the unspoken emotions implicit in another's verbal messages. The following two conversations illustrate the elements of active listening:

Keri: You never take us to the videotape store.

Eric: You don't think I take you to the videotape store often enough.

Keri: Yeah. You never ask us if we would like to go along and pick out some tapes.

Eric: You would like to pick out your own tapes.

Keri: Yeah, could we?

Eric: Sure.

By restating or reflecting Keri's message, Eric was able to help Keri take a more objective look at what she was trying to say. In doing so, Keri was able to discover that not being able to pick out her own tapes was what really disturbed her. In the next example, Linda goes beyond reflecting Jimmy's thoughts to rephrase his unspoken emotions:

Jimmy: I shared my juice with Keri, and now she won't let me ride her bike. I hate Keri.

Linda: Sounds like you're really mad at Keri for not sharing her bike.

Jimmy: No, I don't care about riding her bike. I can't reach the pedals anyway.

Linda: So you just think it's unfair that Keri won't share with you after you shared with her.

Jimmy: Yeah, she's not being fair.

In chapter 1 we discussed the role emotions play in our relationships and the difficulty many people have in identifying and sharing their emotions. Since people often are not aware of how they are feeling, rephrasing their messages can help bring their true feelings to the surface. This is especially helpful when a child has a problem.

Psychologist Thomas Gordon applied Rogers' active listening techniques to develop a unique approach to relating with children. However, Gordon's book *P.E.T.: Parent Effectiveness Training* and his classes have come under heavy criticism for their rejection of parental authority. For example, Gordon writes:

> The stubborn persistence of the idea that parents must and should use authority in dealing with children has, in my opinion, prevented for centuries any significant change or improvement in the way children are raised by parents and treated by adults.[7]

We subscribe to the opposite view regarding parental authority (*see* chapter 4), and we concur with psychologist James Dobson, who contends that Gordon's "antiauthority views are directly contradictory to the teachings of Scripture."[8] However, Dobson accepts, as we do, Gordon's approach to listening skills:

> The most effective aspect of the P.E.T. program involves the teaching of listening skills. Dr. Gordon accurately recognizes the failure of many parents to comprehend what their children are actually saying. They hear the words, of course, but do not discern the true meaning which the child is conveying. The ability to engage in active listening, as it is called, is a valuable skill which should be learned by every parent. I can enthusiastically recommend this feature of Gordon's program.[9]

It is this feature, active listening, that we believe builds intimacy between parents and children. Parents need to develop active listening skills and to apply them daily in their relationship with their children. Your children will tell you everything you need to know about them and their problems, if given a chance. Active listening enables you to give your children that chance.

When to Use Active Listening   The principle of *problem ownership* provides a useful method for recognizing when to use active listening.[10] In his relationship with his parents, a child "owns the problem" when unpleasant experiences result from his unsatisfactory behavior.

Examples of problems owned by the child include:

> Keri thinks dance class is too hard.
> Jimmy is sad because he broke his favorite toy.
> Keri is unable to decide whether she wants to go roller-skating with a friend or go to a neighbor's birthday party.

Jimmy finds it hard to sit in his chair at school.
Keri gets angry when she loses a race to her brother.
Jimmy is upset because Keri is starting kindergarten
and he's not.

In their relationship with their child, parents "own the problem" when their needs are not being satisfied because the child's behavior is interfering in some way. In these situations, the child is meeting his needs, but his behavior bothers, frustrates, or deprives his parents of something.

Examples of situations in which the parent owns the problem include:

Eric is unable to hear the news on the radio because
Jimmy is engaging in vocal play.
Linda is upset because Keri conveniently forgot to
brush her teeth.
Eric is angry because Jimmy has answered back with
a sassy reply.
Linda is hurt because Jimmy has told her a lie.
Eric is frustrated because Keri and Jimmy are ignoring
his directive to clean up their toys.
Linda is unhappy with Keri and Jimmy's whining
behavior.

Situations in which the parent "owns the problem" are best handled within the framework of the disciplinary cycle presented in chapter 4. Situations in which the child "owns the problem" are appropriately managed by the use of active listening. While most children won't openly reveal that they have a problem, few children make a conscious effort to hide the telltale signs: withdrawal and irritability. Parents can help their child gain self-confidence and psychological health by learning to recognize when he is sending an I've-got-a-problem message and help him solve his problem with active listening.

Solving Child-Owned Problems With Active Listening

Unfortunately, active listening is more of an attitude than a technique. A mechanical approach will have a hollow ring and sound insincere. Dr. Gordon cites six attitudes that must be present when using active listening:

1. You must *want* to hear what the child has to say. This means you are willing to take the time to listen. If you don't have time, you need only say so.
2. You must genuinely *want* to be helpful to him with his particular problem at that time. If you don't want to, wait until you do.
3. You must genuinely be able to *accept his feelings*, whatever they may be or however different they may be from your own feelings or from the feelings you think a child "should" feel. This attitude takes time to develop.
4. You must have a deep feeling of *trust* in the child's capacity to handle his feelings, to work through them, and to find solutions to his problems. You will acquire this trust by watching your child solve his own problems.
5. You must appreciate that feelings are *transitory*, not permanent. Feelings change—hate can turn into love, discouragement may quickly be replaced by hope. Consequently, you need not be afraid of feelings getting expressed; they will not become forever fixed inside the child. Active listening will demonstrate this to you.

6. You must be able to see your child as *someone separate* from you—a unique person no longer joined to you, a separate individual having been given by you his *own* life and his *own* identity. This "separateness" will enable you to "permit" the child to have his *own* feelings, his *own* way of perceiving things. Only by feeling "separateness" will you be able to be a helping agent for the child. You must be "with" him as he experiences his problems, but not joined to him.[11]

It is difficult to imagine how parents could fail to establish and maintain an intimate relationship with their child, even without active listening, if they expressed these attitudes. But how can parents acquire these attitudes? In chapter 1 we examined the origin of our attitudes and the role they play in determining our behavior. From this discussion, we learned that we derive our attitudes from our beliefs, and we can change our attitudes by changing our beliefs. Dr. Gordon cites twelve commonly accepted beliefs that prevent us from adopting the attitudes needed for effective active listening. These include accepting as helpful any of the following responses to children who "own a problem":

1. ORDERING, DIRECTING, COMMANDING
   Telling the child to do something; giving him a command.
2. WARNING, ADMONISHING, THREATENING
   Telling the child what consequences will occur if he does something.
3. EXHORTING, MORALIZING, PREACHING
   Telling the child what he *should* or *ought* to do.

4. ADVISING, GIVING SOLUTIONS OR SUG-
    GESTIONS
    Telling the child how to solve a problem; giving
    him advice or suggestions; providing answers
    or solutions for him.

5. LECTURING, TEACHING, GIVING LOGICAL
    ARGUMENTS
    Trying to influence the child with facts, coun-
    terarguments, logic, information, or your own
    opinions.

6. JUDGING, CRITICIZING, DISAGREEING,
    BLAMING
    Making a negative judgment or evaluation of
    the child.

7. PRAISING, AGREEING
    Offering a positive evaluation or judgment;
    agreeing.

8. NAME-CALLING, RIDICULING, SHAMING
    Making the child feel foolish; putting the child
    into a category; shaming him.

9. INTERPRETING, ANALYZING, DIAGNOSING
    Telling the child what his motives are or analyz-
    ing why he is doing or saying something; com-
    municating that you have figured him out or
    have him diagnosed.

10. REASSURING, SYMPATHIZING, CONSOL-
     ING, SUPPORTING
     Trying to make the child feel better; talking him
     out of his feelings; trying to make his feelings go
     away; denying the strength of his feelings.

11. PROBING, QUESTIONING, INTERROGATING
     Trying to find reasons, motives, causes; search-
     ing for more information to help you solve the
     problem.

12. WITHDRAWING, DISTRACTING, HUMOR-
     ING, DIVERTING
     Trying to get the child away from the problem;
     withdrawing from the problem yourself; dis-
     tracting the child; kidding him out of it; pushing
     the problem aside.[12]

Each of these mistaken beliefs about how parents can
help their child solve problems he owns is illustrated in
this dialogue between Eric and Keri:

Eric: It's time to get dressed for dance class.

Keri: I don't want to go to dance class.

Eric: Sure you do. Dance class helps you learn how to
express yourself and develops your coordination [lectur-
ing, teaching, giving logical arguments].

Keri: No, I don't want to go.

Eric: Well, that's a fine attitude. If I had an attitude like
that, we would go hungry around here [judging, criticizing, disagreeing, blaming].

Keri: Do I have to go?

Eric: Yes. Now go put on your leotard [ordering,
directing, commanding].

Keri: But I don't want to go.

Eric: Okay, why don't you want to go [probing, questioning, interrogating]?

Keri: Miss Susan makes us do things that are too hard.

Eric: Well, don't worry. You'll learn to do those difficult steps. And besides, everyone feels that way some-
time. You'll feel different next week [reassuring,
sympathizing, consoling, supporting].

Keri: No I won't. The class is too hard.

Eric: You're just a little anxious because next month is
your dance recital. You don't really think the class is too
hard [interpreting, analyzing, diagnosing].

Keri: Yes I do. I can't do half of what Miss Susan wants me to do.

Eric: Well, I think you're right; some of those steps are hard. But you have the ability to be a good dancer [praising, agreeing].

Keri: No I don't.

Eric: Hey, are you going to be a quitter? You sure sound like a little baby [name-calling, ridiculing, shaming].

Keri: I just don't like dance class.

Eric: If you quit now, you'll be sorry later. If you know what's good for you, you'll stick with it [warning, admonishing, threatening].

Keri: Why do I have to?

Eric: Because it's a commitment. You ought to finish what you start [exhorting, moralizing, preaching].

Keri: Okay, how long do I have to go to dance school?

Eric: Why don't you stick it out until the end of the year. Just a few more months, then you decide if you really want to quit [advising, giving solutions or suggestions].

Keri: Two whole months!

Eric: Come on, go get your leotard on and we'll stop on the way to dance class for a couple of ice-cream cones [withdrawing, distracting, humoring, diverting].

Fortunately, the above conversation never took place. Imagine how frustrating it would be to have someone treat you with such insensitivity. Certainly, you would feel misunderstood and alienated. The conversation that did occur, however, employed active listening to build intimacy between Keri and Eric. That conversation went like this:

Eric: It's time to get dressed for dance class.

Keri: I don't want to go to dance class.

Eric: Oh?

Keri: Miss Susan makes us do things that are too hard.

Eric: You can't do the things Miss Susan asks you to do.

Keri: Yeah. They're too hard. Only Sally and Kathy can do those things.

Eric: Sally and Kathy are better at doing what Miss Susan wants than you are.

Keri: Well, they've been taking lessons since they were three years old. I just started dance class this year.

Eric: It's hard to keep up with two girls who have taken dance classes for three years.

Keri: Yeah, and I feel stupid around them.

Eric: You don't look so good in comparison.

Keri: Yeah, I am trying real hard.

Eric: You're trying to do your best.

Keri: That's all I can do.

Eric: You can't do any more than your best.

Keri: Right! (*leaving to put on her leotard*)

So the competition was getting to Keri. Active listening helped Eric understand Keri's problem and enabled Keri to view her situation objectively and formulate her own solution. Notice the contrast between approaches: In the first conversation, Keri's motivation for not wanting to go to dance class never surfaced. Her feelings of inadequacy were never addressed. Who could blame her for resenting the treatment she received. In the second conversation, Eric's use of active listening gave Keri the opportunity to disclose her feelings and be heard. She left the conversation with positive feelings for Eric and confirmation that her parents are available to help her solve her problems.

The key to building intimacy is the ability to communicate genuine acceptance of another person. Effective parents communicate acceptance of their children by taking time to respond to the interactions they initiate, by being open with their children and sharing their feelings (including apologizing when appropriate), and by using active listening to help children solve their problems.

Acceptance allows children to grow and develop. Unfortunately, the power of acceptance is not widely understood. Many parents fear that if they accept their children, they are somehow communicating it is okay for their children to remain the way they are. To their way of thinking, the best way to help their children develop their potential is to focus on their weaknesses. Consequently, their communication is highly evaluative, judgmental, and critical. This turns kids off. They learn to hide their feelings and problems. They stop talking to their parents altogether.

The Delicate Balance Between Love and Control

Imagine that each year of your child's life is represented by a red leather-bound book. Some books remain blank, waiting for your child to live that year. Now imagine this chapter and the previous chapter as two bookends. By stressing the need to exercise discipline and offering specific suggestions for managing behavior, chapter 4 keeps those precious books from tumbling off one end of the bookshelf. This chapter, with its emphasis on the need to accept your child and its three suggestions for building intimacy, keeps those highly valued books from falling off the other end of the bookshelf. Both approaches are needed to keep those important books from being damaged. Try to make do with just one, and you have a mess.

The central theme of this book is that love and control must be present in successful families. Together love and control create a secure environment in which children can learn to love and respect God, their families, and themselves. Dr. Dobson said it best:

Healthy parenthood can be boiled down to those two essential ingredients, love and control, operating in a system of checks and balances. Any concentration on love to the exclusion of control usually breeds disrespect and contempt. Conversely, an authoritarian and oppressive home atmosphere is deeply resented by the child, who feels unloved or even hated.[13]

6
Building Self-Esteem

He died for us so that, whether we are awake or asleep, we may live together with him. Therefore encourage one another and build each other up, just as in fact you are doing.

1 Thessalonians 5:10, 11 NIV

The Crippling Effects of Inferiority

"Are not five sparrows sold for two pennies? Yet not one of them is forgotten by God. Indeed, the very hairs of your head are all numbered. Don't be afraid; you are worth more than many sparrows" (Luke 12:6, 7 NIV).

Try sharing Luke's assurance of man's worth with a teenage girl who still breathes through her mouth, whose face is covered with pimples, and whose teeth are hidden behind a full set of braces. She looks in the mirror and winces at the loathsome creature she sees. "Maybe I should crawl under a rock," she mutters, as she turns away to face her day. Oh my, how this poor girl needs to realize that the value system she has accepted has nothing to do with God's sense of her worth and importance.

Unhealthy Values

Our children's feelings of inadequacy and inferiority are the result of a widely accepted, totally superficial system of evaluating human worth. This system stresses three false values: attractiveness, competence, and control. These false values underpin a cruel and unforgiving system that passes judgment upon our children, accepting few and rejecting most as unworthy. Here's how this unfair system "stacks the deck" against our children:

Self-Esteem and Attractiveness

Blessed Are the Beautiful There is no doubt that our culture greatly values physical attractiveness. For example, researchers have established that attractive women date more, earn higher grades in college, exercise greater influence over men, and get lighter court sentences.[1] In addition, research indicates that men and women who are considered attractive are perceived as more sociable, strong, sensitive, kind, and interesting than are men and women who are regarded as less attractive.[2] Shorter men have more difficulty finding jobs than do taller men. The starting salaries of men over six feet, two inches tall are 12.4 percent higher than equally qualified applicants under six feet tall.[3]

Moreover, children learn the importance of beauty very early in life. Preschoolers as young as three, for example, were found to agree about who was attractive ("cute") and who was unattractive ("homely") when shown photographs of children their own age. Researchers also found that preschoolers judged by their classmates as pretty were most liked while those judged least pretty were least liked.

Finally, children attributed positive social characteristics ("he's friendly") to those rated good-looking while attributing negative social characteristics ("he hits other children") to those rated unattractive.[4]

Sending the Wrong Message How in the world does a child as young as three learn that beauty counts and attractiveness is the principle that measures human worth? Who told him beauty was important? If he is a Christian, why hasn't he learned that God judges human worth according to a totally different set of values? God never favors beautiful people, as Samuel learned in his search for God's anointed king of Israel: "Do not consider his appearance or his height, for I have rejected him. The Lord does not look at the things man looks at. Man looks at the outward appearance, but the Lord looks at the heart" (1 Samuel 16:7 NIV).

Are you ready for a shock? We teach them. That's right. Oh, we don't set out to instill a false value in children. We don't say, "You count more than Johnny because you're better looking than he is." It's not what we *say*, it's what we *do* that is so instructive. The sad truth is that we adults respond differently to the attractive child than we do to the unattractive child, and the differences in our responses don't go unnoticed by children.

We recently observed two families enter our church together. The first family's three-year-old daughter could be a poster child. Her pleasant features are enhanced by beautiful blond curls and big blue eyes. As she entered the church, the two greeters at the door immediately knelt to her level to establish physical contact. They stroked her head and poked her tummy and raved about her beauty: "Oh, aren't you a cutie pie. I think I'll just take you home with me. And what a pretty dress." Then as the homely four-year-old daughter of the second family entered the church, the greeters stood up, took a step back, and said, "And how are you today?" Both girls learned that the attractive child is the more accepted and valued individual.

It is not surprising, then, that our children are deeply involved in the beauty cult that draws upon its arbitrary and ruthless standards to judge their worth and the worth of their peers. Then as childhood yields to adolescence, the practice intensifies and turns destructive. Failing to look like any of the countless beautiful people they see on television and in the pages of the glamour magazines, preteens and teenagers alike are subjected to a period of intense self-doubt. They walk through the halls of their schools, heads down, hoping no one will notice their imperfect faces and underdeveloped bodies. Lacking confidence in their physical appearance, they are prime targets for those who will urge them to take drugs, give sexual favors, or join a gang of punk rockers.

Self-Esteem and Competence

A second valued personal attribute in our society is the mastery of knowledge or a socially desirable skill. We are a people who devote considerable time and resources to the creation and subsequent worship of superstars. "We're number 1! We're number 1!" scream frenzied sports fans, riding their teams' coattails in the hopes of elevating their own importance. The ability to handle the intellectual and physical world with skill is an important measure of worthiness.

Blessed Are the Intelligent As legislative acts and legal decisions have rendered discrimination based on such attributes as race, religion, sex, and age unlawful, our society is increasingly turning to a new individual trait—intelligence—to create a privileged class. Programs for the gifted child are an established element of public education. Martha Weinman Lear zeros in on our tendency to value the intelligent child more than the average or dull child when she observes, "By the present line of thinking all children deserve the very best except the gifted, who deserve even better."[5]

It is not surprising, then, that children gauge their self-worth according to how smart they believe they are. Evidence of this unfortunate tendency was provided by Pauline Sears and Vivian Sherman, who studied ten-year-old children over a period of two years. Changes in their scholastic achievement resulted in considerable changes in their self-esteem. Children who improved their academic performance experienced increased self-esteem; children who failed to improve their academic performance experienced decreased self-esteem.[6]

Since the exceptionally intelligent child is just that—an exception—the bulk of children are vulnerable to low self-esteem. As we are teachers ourselves, we know that the school environment provides little in the way of ego support for the average and below-average child. Seeing himself in a low reading group (the Blackbirds), suffering the humiliation of being the first one spelled down in a spelling bee, enduring the embarrassment of being the last one chosen to compete in a math contest—little Johnny is an easy mark for those who want him to skip school, smoke a joint in the boys' room, or shoplift something from the local discount store.

Blessed Are the Athletic   Children can gain a sense of competence by mastery of sport as well as academic subjects. Our society assigns high status to those who can put a ball through a hoop, run one hundred yards without being tackled, or kick a soccer ball into a net. But when it comes to deriving high self-esteem from athletic ability, there is good news and bad news. The good news is that the talented athlete doesn't even have to be handsome or smart. The bad news is that athletic ability is not distributed equitably in the population, and unlike physical appearance, which can be enhanced by everything from wardrobe to cosmetic surgery, either you have athletic talent or you don't. Sure, coaching helps. But good coaching doesn't make superstars!

There is another problem: Nature has put every child's physical development on a separate timetable. Since success in so many sports is dependent on size and strength as well as agility, late-maturing children are often robbed of the high self-esteem they could have derived from early athletic skill. Paul Mussen and Mary Jones documented the plight of the late-maturers. Studying seventeen-year-old boys, they found that late-maturers displayed less favorable self-concepts than did early-maturers.[7] The same researchers reported similar findings for seventeen-year-old girls.[8] Once again, a large segment of children are shut out, unable to develop their self-esteem by demonstrating intellectual or athletic competence, two personal attributes highly valued by their peers.

Self-Esteem and Control

Our society values the ability to manage impulsive behavior. Those who can comply with the appropriate moral and ethical standards of conduct are held in high esteem. We characterize adults who successfully control their behavior as well-mannered, refined, or gracious. We characterize children who successfully control their behavior as "neat kids."

Blessed Are the Emotionally Mature   Silly and excitable children have a tough time with both their peers and adults. Kids love to laugh and run wild, but they also have a serious side. The attention-seeking class clown is apt to receive more ridicule than laughs.

The negative effects of uncontrolled behavior were studied by Pauline Sears and Vivian Sherman. These researchers found that among ten-year-old children, changes in socially desirable behavior were closely related to changes in self-esteem. Children whose behavior became more socially desirable increased their self-esteem, while children whose behavior became less socially desirable decreased their self-esteem.[9]

The controlled child gets more support and positive feedback from adults than does the uncontrolled child. Such a response sets up a vicious cycle: The mature get more mature and the immature get more immature. The child who is waiting for changes in his body chemistry to quiet his excitable nature finds no opportunity to draw upon his personality to build high self-esteem. He lies like a sitting duck, susceptible to the suggestion that he pull a dumb stunt, get drunk, or run away from home.

Healthy Values

Every child needs to belong somewhere. When children identify with their peer group, they buy into an unfair system that assigns human worth to those who are attractive, competent, or controlled. As we have already seen, few can capitalize on these personal attributes. The worth and dignity of only a handful are affirmed by this system. Most are punished for their plain, ordinary appearance; moderate to low intelligence; impulsive, unsophisticated behavior—unless, of course, they conform. The peer group grants clemency to those willing to compromise themselves and go along with the crowd.

Children of accepting parents often avoid the injustice of a system that apportions worth only to those who measure up to a set of superficial values. Accepting parents affirm their children's worth by loving them unconditionally. Unconditional love attaches no strings to the giving and receiving of affection and care. Parents who love unconditionally avoid explicit and implicit messages that say, "I love you if . . ." and "I love you when. . . ." Instead, parents who love unconditionally communicate messages that say, "You don't need to be anything or do anything in order for me to love you. If you become something I value or you do something I value, I'll be happy for you, but I won't love you any more than I already do. I love you because you are you." When supported by unconditional love, children of accepting parents tend to identify themselves with their family and not with their peer group, thereby reducing the pressures to conform.

Accepting parents relate to their children within a system of healthy values. They respect and value themselves, their children, and all people as God's creations—each equally endowed with worth and dignity. Accepting parents respect and value the ability of their children and all people to create and communicate personal meaning and to make their own decisions. Accepting parents respect and value the ability of their children and all people to solve their own problems.

Putting Healthy Values Into Parental Communication

Six bipolar categories of communication identified by psychologist Jack Gibb illustrate how accepting parents send messages that reflect the healthy values presented above.[10] Gibb observed communication in small groups for several years to identify confirming and disconfirming behavior. In his study, Gibb identified six contrasting behaviors as the means by which one can confirm or reject the worth of others:

1. *Evaluation vs. description.* The first type of disconfirming behavior Gibb reported was *evaluation.* Evaluative language often contains an accusatory use of the word *you:*

"You're not being careful."

"You spoiled brat."

"You bad boy."

Not surprisingly, most people resent judgmental statements and interpret them as a lack of respect. By avoiding evaluative statements, affirming parents communicate that they respect and value their children as God's creations.

Gibb offers *descriptive* communication as a desirable alternative to evaluative statements. Descriptive communication explains the impact that another's action has on the speaker. Focusing attention on the effects of another's behavior requires a shift from "you" statements to "I" statements. As a result, messages sound less judgmental.

For example, a parent using descriptive statements might say, "This is the second time a glass of milk has been spilled on the table [description statement]. I am wondering if you're so excited about seeing your friends after lunch that you're not watching what your hands are doing [interpretation statement]. I am getting tired of having to stop eating while you clean up spilled milk [feeling statement]." In this example, in addition to explaining the effects of another's actions, the speaker interprets the other's actions and expresses his feelings as well.

What Gibb treats as one category of communication, our DIFFER format treats as three categories: *description, interpretation,* and *feeling* (*see* chapter 1). We separated Gibb's *evaluation vs. description* category into its component parts to assist affirming parents in applying this communication principle to the important task of conveying love and respect to their children.

Perhaps additional examples would be helpful. Keri and Jimmy are now grade-schoolers, but we can imagine this situation (and the situations to follow) occurring during their teenage years: Keri has been bothered by the pressure of school and problems with her boyfriend. If Linda confronted Keri using evaluative communication, her statements might sound like this:

"[crossly] Keri, you haven't been fit to live with lately. You've been so thoughtless and hostile. You've been ignoring your schoolwork and running around with a lot of loud and ill-mannered friends."

Confronting Keri using description would probably evoke a more positive response. The contrasting approach would sound something like this:

"[sensitively] Keri, I don't know what's been happening between us lately, but I've been deeply hurt by some of the exchanges we've had."

2. *Control vs. problem orientation.* The second type of disconfirming behavior Gibb notes is *control*. Attempts to control others usually involve imposing decisions upon them with little regard for their ideas, needs, or interests. Like children, some adults take power trips simply to enhance their egos. Controlling parents generate resentment in their children by communicating the message, "You do as I say because I know what's best for you. Otherwise, we're going to have problems."

The affirming parent opts for the contrasting behavior, *problem orientation.* This does not impose a previously made decision on another person. Instead, problem-oriented communication invites another to participate in the decision-making process. Our DIFFER format contains no statements comparable to Gibb's problem orientation category. So here is a new tool for affirming parents who want to communicate respect for their child's ability to solve problems and make decisions.

Suppose as a teenager, Keri has spent many hours planning her high school course schedule. She then presents the courses she has selected to her father for his approval.

Keri: I think I'll take Earth Science 100 with Mr. Waters.

A response strong on control might sound like this:

Eric: You don't want a course in earth science. You want a course in one of the basic sciences—physics or chemistry. You want a course of substance.

Imagine the demoralizing effects of such a controlling message. On the other hand, Eric could respond with the following problem-oriented message:

Eric: Before locking into a course in earth science, how can we assure that your program of study will include rigorous courses as well?

3. *Strategy vs. spontaneity. Strategy* or manipulation is one of the more commonly used types of disconfirming communication. Children often try to trick others into doing something for them. Unfortunately, many adults never outgrow this approach. When parents are strategic with their children, children learn to mistrust their parents.

Spontaneity avoids bad feelings with candid and honest statements. Direct requests for what is sought replace manipulation in spontaneous communication. Although the word *spontaneity* suggests impulsive and immediate communication of ideas, the chief characteristic defining this category is honesty. A person can plan the wording of his message in great detail and still be spontaneous, so long as he is honest about what he is after. Our DIFFER format contains no category similar to spontaneity; so here is another new tool for affirming parents.

Let's say that Jimmy is now a teenager and Eric doesn't approve of Jimmy's friends. As summer approaches, Eric attempts to reduce the time Jimmy will spend with them. Using strategy, he confronts Jimmy as follows:

Eric: Hey Jimmy, how would you like to take some computer classes this summer?

Jimmy: Wow, can I?

Eric: Sure can. In fact, why don't you take a couple of courses, or even three.

Jimmy: Gee, that's a lot of school.

Eric: Well, not if you stay with your uncle in St. Louis. You would have lots of time for computer classes.

Jimmy: My uncle in St. Louis?

Eric: Sure. St. Louis University has a great summer program in computer science especially for high school students. Of course, you would have to register for the whole summer. What do you say?

Jimmy: The whole summer?

Eric: Yep!

Jimmy: !§£$%&

If you were Jimmy, wouldn't you feel as if you were being suckered into doing something you didn't want to do? Nobody likes being duped. Wouldn't it be better for Eric to achieve his goal by using spontaneity, as illustrated below:

Eric: Son, I am uncomfortable with the amount of time you spend with your friends. I know you enjoy their company, but I don't think they share your interests.

Jimmy: You don't like my friends?

Eric: Well, whether or not I like your friends really isn't important. What I am saying is that I don't know what you're getting from your friends. Your abilities and interests are different from theirs.

Jimmy: You think I should drop my friends.

Eric: No, but I think you should make some new friends. I would like to suggest that you take some computer classes at St. Louis University this summer. You could stay with your uncle and enroll in as many as three courses.

Jimmy: Okay, I'll consider it.

Affirming parents communicate respect for their children when they use spontaneity. Honest and direct communication tells a child his parents believe he is sufficiently mature to make good decisions and solve difficult problems.

4. *Neutrality vs. empathy.* Gibb's term *neutrality* refers to the various forms of indifference that people communicate. Neutral statements are disconfirming because they communicate that another's welfare doesn't matter. It is deflating to sense that another person doesn't sense the pain we feel or doesn't care if our problems are solved.

Empathy has a contrasting effect on us. Our worth and importance are confirmed when people care about us and our problems. We empathize by accepting another's feelings and imagining how we would feel if we were in their place. Often we can best communicate empathy nonverbally, by putting our arms around someone or holding his hand. Our DIFFER format contains no category identical to empathy, so here is an additional type of message that parents might employ when they are seeking to affirm their children.

Here is a situation that most parents have experienced: Their teenager gets a driver's license and has an accident before the end of the week. Let's say Keri had a fender

bender in the family car, and when she approached Eric
with the bad news, he responded with neutrality:

Keri: I've got some bad news.

Eric: Oh?

Keri: I damaged the car.

Eric: (*after finding out if Keri is okay*) Well, before you
drive it again, you'll have to pay for the damage you did.

Keri: But I don't have any money.

Eric: Too bad. Everyone has problems.

Compare this cold and indifferent treatment to the
following empathic response:

Keri: I damaged the car.

Eric: (*after finding out if Keri is okay*) Well, nobody likes
having an accident. I know it always unnerves me when I
have a wreck.

Keri: I am so upset.

Eric: I bet you are rattled. But you know, you are
responsible for the damage you did. Before you can drive
the car again, you'll have to pay the repair bill.

Keri: But I don't have any money.

Eric: I think I know how you feel. This month I had
two bills I couldn't pay and still afford the lawn mower
I've been wanting to buy. It's hard to do without while
saving your money.

In this example, while Eric held Keri to meeting her
responsibilities, he also conveyed the message that she
mattered to him by communicating concern for her
feelings. Empathy is a powerful confirmation tool that
affirming parents use frequently. Even parents of preschoolers can make good use of this communication
category. When Keri comes crying to Linda after a fight
with Jimmy, it often turns out that she's just after a little
empathy. After telling her tale of woe, Keri goes away

satisfied if Linda responds, "Nobody likes to get hit. I'll bet that hurt."

5. *Superiority vs. equality.* The fifth disconfirming behavior cited by Gibb is *superiority.* When a person communicates superiority, he signals that he wants a relationship in which the other person accepts his perceived higher status. When disconfirming parents communicate superiority, they go beyond claiming the higher status accorded them by their parental role. "Look," they imply to their children, "even if we weren't your parents and even if we weren't older, we would be better than you."

Messages of *equality* communicate that even though the speaker has higher status, he sees others as having just as much worth because they are human beings. The affirming parent who communicates equality conveys to his children that he regards them as equally endowed with worth and dignity. Our DIFFER format lacks a category similar to equality, so affirming parents might want to consider including this new category in their communication style.

In the following examples, Linda questions Jimmy about his grades at the end of his freshman year in high school. Acting as a disconfirming parent, her conversation with him might sound like this:

Linda: What did you get in English?

Jimmy: I got a C$^-$.

Linda: A C$^-$. I got an A$^+$ when I took freshman English.

On the other hand, enacting the role of a confirming parent, her conversation with Jimmy would sound something like this:

Linda: A C$^-$. But you seem to know quite a lot. And your teacher says you talk well in class, too.

6. *Certainty vs. provisionalism.* The last category of disconfirming behavior Gibb termed *certainty.* He observed that some people act as if they have all the facts. Because they think they know it all, they insist that their opinions, in fact, are truths. These are people who believe their way is the only way to do things. Their disregard for the thoughts of others undermines the self-confidence of those with whom they relate.

Affirming parents, however, enact *provisionalism* to promote their children's self-esteem. They are willing to admit they don't have all the answers. They are open to new information and are willing to change their minds if the arguments their children present are sensible. Our DIFFER format does not include a category like provisionalism, so here is another communication tool for affirming your children.

The process by which a family makes everyday decisions illustrates this category of communication. If Eric were to enact certainty, the conversation might sound something like this:

Jimmy: Where are we going to eat tonight?

Eric: McDonald's, of course.

Jimmy: How about that new place on One Hundred Forty-fourth Street?

Eric: No, we're eating at McDonald's.

What is Eric saying in the above example? "Your ideas are not worth considering," is the implicit message. Compare the deflating effects of certainty to the confirming messages implicit in provisional communication.

Eric: There are many places we could eat. Let's list them and consider each separately.

Jimmy: How about that new place on One Hundred Forty-fourth Street?

Eric: Okay. Any other ideas?

Provisionalism enables affirming parents to send confirming messages to their children. By being open to new information, affirming parents are saying, "I respect your ability to generate and communicate useful ideas."

Assessing Your Child's Self-Esteem

Each child holds a set of perceptions about himself. If a child sees himself positively, we say he has high *self-esteem*. Skillful use of the six categories of supportive communication identified by Gibb should create a climate in which children develop high levels of self-esteem. Parents can gauge the positive effects of the healthy values imparted through supportive communication by monitoring the frequency with which their children enact *defense mechanisms*. These are ways of avoiding the reality of who we are in favor of a more positive identity. Each defense mechanism presented below represents a specific way in which children distort reality so they can perceive themselves more positively.

Table 1 defines twelve commonly used defense mechanisms and presents an example for each.[11] To gauge the effectiveness of your supporting communication, rate the frequency with which your children enact each defense mechanism, checking for (1) low-level use, (2) moderate-level use, and (3) high-level use. A total score of twenty-eight or above indicates a need for increased supportive communication.

TABLE 1
An Inventory of Defense Mechanisms

Mechanism	Frequency		

1. **Rationalization**
   Definition: To think up logical but untrue reasons one's behavior was acceptable.
   Example: Shrugging off failing to clean up by saying, "I was too busy."   1   2   3

2. **Compensation**
   Definition: To stress a strength in an area, hoping to hide a shortcoming.
   Example: Devoting a great deal of time to developing an athletic skill to hide low academic skills.   1   2   3

3. **Reaction Formation**
   Definition: To avoid facing a problem by acting just the opposite of how one really feels.
   Example: Saying, "I am glad I didn't make the team. Now I can spend more time with my friends."   1   2   3

4. **Projection**
   Definition: To put the blame for a shortcoming on someone or something else.
   Example: Claiming someone made the child late getting home because he didn't have a watch.   1   2   3

5. **Identification**
   Definition: To hide shortcomings by imitating someone the child admires.
   Example: Saying, "I look and act like a rock star, and rockers don't care if they can do math either."   1   2   3

6. **Fantasy**
   Definition: To daydream oneself into a more acceptable world.
   Example: Thinking that since the father on a soap opera works late because he dislikes his family, when one's father works late, he's signaling his dislike for the family.   1   2   3

Mechanism	Frequency		
7. **Repression** Definition: To deny the existence of a short-coming. Example: Pretending to be able to read when one can't.	1	2	3
8. **Dependency or Regression** Definition: To convince oneself one can't do something when, in reality, one doesn't want to do something. Example: Saying, "I'd love to read that story, but I don't have time," when one has time but is ashamed of low reading skills.	1	2	3
9. **Apathy** Definition: To avoid getting hurt by not getting involved. Example: Refusing to study for a test because of fear of failure.	1	2	3
10. **Displacement** Definition: To be aggressive toward people who are less threatening than the person who caused the anger originally. Example: The child who is angry with his mother but takes his anger out on his sister.	1	2	3
11. **Undoing** Definition: To offer a symbolic apology in place of admitting one was wrong. Example: Being helpful around the house instead of apologizing after a shouting match.	1	2	3
12. **Verbal Aggression** Definition: Drowning out criticism. Example: Shouting abusive statements after having been reprimanded.	1	2	3

Perhaps you recognize some of these defense mechanisms in your child's behavior. If so, you are probably seeing perfectly normal behavior (unless your child has scored above twenty-eight on the preceding inventory). Highly defensive children are symptomatic of disconfirming communication. The following dialogue in which a college-age Keri confronts her mother with her weekend plans illustrates how nonsupportive communication draws defensive behavior from children:

Keri: Mom, I might go down to Kansas City this weekend.

Linda: You're going where?

Keri: I might go to Kansas City.

Linda: Who are you going with and where do you plan to stay?

Keri: Oh, I'll probably go with Sally from school, and we'll find a place to stay.

Linda: You're not going to go down there until I know where you're going to stay [certainty].

Keri: (annoyed) I am going to Kansas City, okay! [verbal aggression].

Linda: Don't you talk to me in that tone of voice! [control].

Keri: But Mother, I'm going to Kansas City to see the art museum, and I want to stop in Lawrence on the way home to see Aunt Pat [rationalization].

Linda: I seriously doubt if you're going to see an art museum. I love and appreciate art, but you don't know a Picasso from a Rembrandt. And your aunt Pat lives in Lawrence, Missouri, not in Lawrence, Kansas [superiority].

Keri: Look, Mother. I'm tired of being treated like a three-year-old child. Why don't you let me grow up and stop being the overprotective, neurotic, maternal menace you are! I mean really, Mother, why don't you just get off my case! [verbal aggression].

Linda: Well, you're a sassy, spoiled brat to talk to me that way [evaluation].

Jimmy (enters through the back door) Keri, can I use your portable radio?

Keri: No, and I don't want you snooping around my room, either, you little creep [displacement].

Linda: Well, Keri, I don't care how angry you get. You're not going to Kansas City [neutrality].

Keri: Mom, I wouldn't have to scream and shout at you if you would listen to me and be reasonable [projection].

Linda: Keri, let's eat out and go to a movie tonight. You'll feel better about this in the morning, you'll see [strategy].

Keri: Oh, I don't care if I get to Kansas City. In fact, I don't care about anything [reaction formation].

Look at the destructive effects of disconfirming communication on a child's self-esteem. Who could blame Keri if she turned from her family and identified with her peer group instead? But suppose Linda had been committed to operating from healthy values. Had Linda responded to Keri's plans to go to Kansas City with supportive communication, their conversation might have gone as follows:

Keri: I might go down to Kansas City.

Linda: You would like to go to Kansas City this weekend [description].

Keri: I am thinking about going.

Linda: You know, sweetheart, I don't think I am ready for my daughter to make her own decisions, although I know you're growing up fast [spontaneity].

Keri: I'll be all right, Mom.

Linda: You're probably feeling as if I don't trust your judgment. I know you want to get out on your own now. But I would be a lot more comfortable if I knew who you were going with and where you plan to stay [empathy and spontaneity].

Keri: Oh, I'll probably go with Sally from school, and we'll find a place to stay.

Linda: Well, I suppose there are many places you

could stay. I'll bet you have thought of possible places already [provisionalism].

Keri: Well, Sally's roommate lives in Kansas City.

Linda: That sounds like a good place to stay. I wonder how you could be sure it would be all right for you to stay with her [problem orientation].

Keri: I guess we could call her.

Linda: Fine. You're ready to be on your own, aren't you? Have a great time in Kansas City [equality].

Gibb's six categories of supportive communication are invaluable tools for sending implicit messages of love and respect. Once mastered, the six categories become habitual, and their frequent use builds your child's self-esteem. In addition to covert supportive messages, affirming parents send overt messages of love and respect.

It is shocking how many parents find it difficult, if not impossible, to say to their children, "I love you." The bumper sticker that asks, "Have You Hugged Your Child Today?" says we live in an emotionally crippled society. We kiss and hug our Keri and Jimmy until they protest. That way we're sure they are getting the affection they need for emotional health. Maybe they'll grow up to regard us as pests, but they'll not resent remote and distant parents.

The same parents who find it difficult to express love and affection often find it difficult to praise children as well. Our hearts go out to children who rarely receive praise. We have followed many parents with two or three kids in tow around the grocery store listening in agony to their constant negative directives and comments: "Don't touch those apples! I said don't touch those apples! What's the matter with you? Are you stupid or something? I said don't touch those apples! [Goes over, slaps the kid's hand, and shakes him until his teeth rattle.] I said don't touch those apples [throws the kid in the cart]; now sit in there and don't you dare get out."

Okay, we don't want our kids to touch the apples either. But in addition to saying no to touching the apples, we make an effort to praise our children for their compliance. "Good job keeping your hands to yourself," we say as we move from aisle to aisle. Our rule of thumb is to give as much praise to our children as we give criticism.

In addition to building self-esteem, praising children reinforces desirable behavior. In this way, praise operates as a disciplinary tool. It is important, however, to praise the task rather than the child. Saying, "What a good boy you are," or worse yet, "Mommy loves you," to reinforce the child's cleaning his room suggests to the child that your love for him is conditional. Since Mommy loves him regardless of how his room looks, it is more appropriate to say, "Boy, this room looks great. When you keep your room clean, you can find the things you're looking for, and things don't get broken as easily."

Can you overpraise a child? Yes. Unlike expressions of love, excessive compliments can be ineffective and, in some cases, destructive. Writer Joel Shurkin shares seven guidelines to help parents praise their children effectively. According to Shurkin, research indicates that compliments are most effective when parents praise:

1. Genuine progress or accomplishment.
2. Acts in which children are unaware of how well they have done.
3. Acts for which children are not seeking praise through manipulation.
4. In varied and unique ways, not automatically.
5. In a nonintrusive and natural manner.
6. Both effort and ability.

7.   Activity to achieve those goals that the children
     value.[12]

The family is the key to building children's self-esteem.
Affirming parents make their children feel good about
themselves and the families in which they live. By their
implicit and explicit confirming messages, parents take the
pressure off their kids to try to win the approval of their
peer group.

7
Forming Values and Acquiring Life Skills

Train a child in the way he should go, and when he
is old he will not turn from it.

Proverbs 22:6 NIV

Nobody said being a parent was going to be easy! In
addition to managing discipline, establishing intimacy,
and building self-esteem, effective parents endow their
children with the values and life skills they will need to
make decisions. You are responsible for giving your
children the tools they need to critically evaluate their
options and exercise good judgment. The time and effort
you invest today toward developing value consciousness
and life skills in your child will pay large dividends
tomorrow.

Values Caught Not Taught

Teaching the virtues of various desirable qualities and
proven principles turns kids off and invites rebellion.
Why? Because teaching messages contain implicit statements of control and certainty (*see* chapter 6). Instead of
undermining a child's confidence and self-esteem with
disconfirming statements, why not take advantage of a
universal characteristic of children: close and continual
scrutiny of their parents. Like it or not, your children are
constantly watching you. Little escapes their critical eyes.
Kids want to know about their world—how it works and
what makes it go. You are their window to the adult
world.

Psychologist Jerome Bruner describes the learning process as consisting of two elements: concept formation and concept attainment. *Concept formation* occurs when children can use words to define a concept. The use of dictionary definitions is a form of concept formation. Having a child tell you that courage is acting in spite of the fear he feels indicates he has formed the concept. *Concept attainment* occurs when a child can identify the concept by, in effect, pointing it out. Having a child tell you that his going up to the front of the church for children's worship took courage indicates he has attained the concept.[1]

By living our values, we enable our children to attain and form value concepts—a sound educational strategy. No doubt we would much rather preach our values than model them for our children. But children will not attain value concepts unless they see their parents' values in operation. Table 2 presents sixteen values and the ways we try to live them in our home:

TABLE 2
Values and Activities

1. Rely on God.	Praying together. Allowing our children to observe us taking our problems and concerns to the Lord.
2. Accept your imperfection.	Saying it is okay to make mistakes. Admitting our own mistakes and asking for forgiveness (especially from our children, when we've made disciplinary mistakes).
3. Accept imperfection in others.	Avoiding and rejecting put-downs. Forgiving those who ask our forgiveness.
4. Live an ordered life.	Assigning chores and insisting that work come before play.

5.	Take responsibility.	Holding family members accountable for their actions: repair or replace what you damage, be on time for dinner or you don't eat, and so forth.
6.	Respect authority.	Seeking God's will. Obeying parents, teachers, and supervisors.
7.	See things in perspective.	Realizing that the importance of what seems so disturbing today will fade tomorrow. Establishing priorities.
8.	Accept conflict.	Not trying to please everyone. Agreeing to disagree.
9.	Manage your emotions.	Realizing emotions are variable and subject to change. Delaying reaction when emotions run high.
10.	Accept change.	Taking our children's growth and development into account when setting rules. Keeping up with technological innovation: learning to use computers.
11.	Develop relationships.	Looking for ways to meet the needs of others. Treating others as we wish to be treated.
12.	Exercise stewardship.	Returning a portion of our income to the Lord. Respecting our environment: picking up trash and disposing of household chemicals properly.
13.	Learn all you can.	Reading to our children. Making sure they see us reading. Attending lectures and concerts.
14.	Avoid materialism.	Curtailing our consumption. Living a simple life.
15.	Take care of your body.	Eating a balanced diet. Exercising regularly. Following the doctor's orders when sick. Getting annual physicals and semiannual dental checkups.
16.	Avoid overcommitment.	Saying no, even to church work, if added responsibility will keep us from enjoying our family.

Life Skills

Life can be pretty confusing. Most kids want to know: How does it all work? What leads to success and what leads to failure? Unfortunately, we parents are not always forthcoming with the information our children need to live effective lives. It's sad, really, because they depend on us for a knowledge of basics in the areas of sexuality, adolescence, and adulthood.

Understanding Sexuality

Some parents wait too long before talking about sex with their children, hoping they will never need to know. Then they opt for a crash course. Others never talk to their children about sex. Nevertheless, these same parents teach their children about sex through their attitudes. If they believe sex is dirty and shameful, their children will learn sex is dirty and shameful. If they are embarrassed by sexual matters, their children will learn to be embarrassed by sexual matters. There is no escaping the silent messages of nonverbal communication.

Like it or not, children are going to learn sexual lessons from you, their parents. The question you must answer is not, "Are we going to teach our children about sex?" but rather, "Are we going to plan our children's sex education, or just let it happen haphazardly?" If you are going to take a planned approach to sex education, you will need to talk about sex with your children at each phase of their development. Your goals in these discussions should be threefold:

1. Enabling your children to master the facts of sexuality.
2. Developing comfortable attitudes to help your children enjoy themselves as sexual beings.

3. Presenting principled practices to assure that your children will respect the sexuality of others.

Presenting the Facts Before starting to teach your children about sex, you need to be sure you know the facts yourself. If your sex education is typical, you will need to fill in some gaps before trying to answer your child's questions. Christian parents seeking a sensitive presentation of sexual facts will find Dr. Grace H. Ketterman's book *How to Teach Your Child About Sex* a great help.[2]

Both babies and parents love to play "name the body parts." In this game, parents point to a part of the body and ask, "What's this?" and then answer, "That's your ears, toes, or hair." Why not include the genitals in this game, using the correct names? Deliberate avoidance of the sexual organs will not go unnoticed by the child. Naming what lies between the waist and the knees conveys the parents' acceptance of the child's sexuality and provides the child with the correct words for his anatomy.

It is not uncommon for a child of three or four, upon seeing a pregnant woman, to ask how the baby got into its mother's tummy. Fielding your children's questions can be awkward and uncomfortable. Our DIFFER format can put both you and your child at ease. If Jimmy were to ask, "Do babies come out of a mommy's belly button?" Linda might reply as follows:

"You want to know where babies come out of mommies when they are born [interpretation statement]. I'm glad you're interested in knowing how babies are born. Remember how a baby grows in its mommy's womb? Well, when it is ready to be born. . . ."

Helping Children Feel Comfortable Be sure you convey a sense of wonder and joy as you tell your children of the amazing process of procreation. And watch the response your children make to the facts you relate to them. Go at their pace. If their eyes wander or they become restless, stop and continue the story when they ask again. Telling your children about their bodies communicates the message that you accept them as sexual beings. The next step is to send messages that tell your children you accept the ways they are sexual beings.

Once your children get the message that you accept them as sexual beings and you accept their acting on their sexuality, you need to send a final message: Tell your children you expect them to manage their sexual behavior appropriately and responsibly.

Parents, tell your children that unclean thoughts will pop into their heads and they will face a decision each time such thoughts occur. They can dwell on and enlarge these thoughts, or they can do as Paul suggests—dismiss their unclean thoughts and flee sexual immorality. Warn your children that the decision to dwell on their sexual thoughts later can lead to guilt feelings about marital intercourse. But reassure them that deciding to put unclean thoughts out of their minds will allow them to enjoy sex, without guilt, as a gift from God. Having unclean thoughts is not sinful; it is what we do with them that is sinful. Parents, make this point clear to your children.

In addition to addressing the need to control sexual thoughts, you will need to talk frankly to your children about the importance of respecting the sexuality of others. Sex play between children provides the opportunity for you to discuss their obligation to respect the sexuality of others. Since there are no observable harmful effects to body exploration, and sex play appears to be a universal behavior, parents need not make an uproar about it.

Instead, gently pull aside the children who are involved and explain that it is perfectly natural for them to be interested in other people's bodies. However, suggest that their undressing each other or touching each other can lead to uncomfortable or upsetting feelings. Also suggest that until they get older it is difficult for them to tell when someone doesn't care about their feelings and is taking advantage of them.

Offer to explain to your children what they want to know about other people's bodies. Making these statements can be difficult, but our DIFFER format will help put everyone at ease, as illustrated by this exchange between Linda and Keri and her friends:

"I see you children are playing doctor and Keri is the patient because she's gotten undressed [description statement]. I'll bet you're interested in seeing each other without clothes [interpretation statement]. I'm glad you're interested to see how you are the same and how you are different from one another [feeling statement]. But undressing and touching each other can lead to uncomfortable feelings, and sometimes it's hard for us to tell if the kids we're playing with really care about our feelings or if they just want to take advantage of us [effect statements]. Now Keri, I'll be happy to tell you about other people's bodies; Billy and Susie, you can ask your parents if you want to know about other people's bodies. That way you won't have to undress and touch one another. Since you can find out what you want to know from your parents, I want you to know that if you undress or touch each other, I will send everyone home [result statement]."

As your children grow older, encourage them to think about whether or not they have taken sexual advantage of someone, and whether someone has taken sexual advantage of them. If your children express a wish to discuss their thoughts on sexual exploitation, openly discuss the topic with them.

As children grow and approach adolescence, parents should caution them that sexual contact is progressive and very difficult to limit once begun. If children are to exercise sexual responsibility, they need to understand the forces of human psychology and physiology that will propel them to ever higher levels of involvement. The psychological effects of familiarity work to accelerate sexual activity. As we become more physically intimate with another person, we become less inhibited. The physiological effects of acclimatization requires increasing contact and involvement to excite each other. Having explained these factors, invite your children to make a commitment to themselves to restrict their sexual activity to moderate levels of involvement.

Avoiding Sexual Abuse

Parents want their children to grow up in a safe and secure world. Unfortunately, no such environment exists. The world is full of sick people who prey on innocent and unsuspecting children. Occasionally the very people parents trust the most—each other, grandparents, uncles and aunts, friends, and neighbors—turn out to be child abusers. The plain truth is that parents can never know who to trust. The only effective form of protection is to prepare children to respond appropriately if something unexpected happens.

Talking about sexual abuse is difficult because it requires that you confront children with the shadow side of life. Most parents want their children to remain innocent for as long as possible. Telling them that they are potential victims of some sick adult is very painful. In addition, we want our children to feel comfortable about sexuality, not frightened by it.

Responsible parents, however, face the facts and prepare their children to respond effectively to potential sex abuse. The first step is to be sure your children know their rights. Children need to be told that their bodies belong to them, not to someone else, and that no one has the right to see or touch their bodies, unless they say it's okay. Children should also be told to trust their feelings, and if someone makes them feel uncomfortable, to say, "Stop, I don't like that!" They should be coached to act on their feelings and to move away or run if someone ignores their feelings and continues to make them uncomfortable.

Educating children regarding sexual abuse cannot be done effectively in one shot. Lectures need to be reinforced through as many teaching moments as possible. For example, if Eric saw Keri talking to a stranger in a shopping center, he would pull Keri aside and, using our DIFFER format, gently remind her of the danger she faced:

"I saw you talking to that man [description statement]. I wonder if you've forgotten how dangerous it is to talk to strangers [interpretation statement]. It really worries me that you didn't just walk away from that man [feeling statement]. He probably was just being friendly, but what if he wanted to get you out of the store and into his car? You could have been in big trouble then [effect statement]. The next time I see you being friendly with strangers, we'll leave the store and go home [result statement]."

Understanding Adolescence

Keri and Jimmy are now seven and six years old, respectively. That leaves us a few years before the onset of puberty. But already we're running scared. Our friends tell us their tales of woe, describing the turbulent and painful exchanges that are undermining their family life. We hold their hands and assure them that this too will pass and life will someday return to normal. But we know that soon it will be our turn. What then?

We have adopted a first-strike policy that entails two lines of attack: First, raise well-adjusted kids and issue lots of storm warnings. We figure if Keri and Jimmy enter puberty psychologically sound and socially adjusted, they will be better able to ride the whirlwind. We are working hard during these early years to establish respect for authority, develop intimacy, and build Keri's and Jimmy's self-esteem. We know that once the happy hormones kick in, everything goes up for grabs. We know that kids who enter puberty lost and wounded might plummet into a void five to seven years later as adulthood approaches. But our hope is that when the dust settles, Keri and Jimmy can start where they left off.

Our second line of attack is to engage Keri and Jimmy in several in-depth discussions about the changes and possibly frightening experiences they will face one or two years before they occur. Our goal is to inoculate them against ignorance, fear, and confusion. We have both lived through puberty, and we know how frightening and upsetting those years can be. Why not share our experiences with our children? We also have a great deal of information at our disposal that can enlighten Keri and Jimmy. Why not lay out the whole program—tell them what's going to happen, when it's going to happen, why it's going to happen, and when it's going to be over. Here's how we plan to hold those in-depth discussions:

Make 'em Feel Special   Convention planners, as a rule, hold their meetings in exciting cities. Location is important in getting people to attend, but location also puts participants in the right frame of mind. Often participants never leave the hotel—just being in New Orleans or San Francisco lifts their spirits. So why not invite your preteen to pick from two or three places that are acceptable to you, and go away for your talks. In addition to making the experience exciting, going away takes you out of the everyday turmoil of family life, allowing you to focus all your attention on your preteen. Plan to be away two or three days. That will give you time to cover all the bases and time for your preteen to reflect on your words of wisdom.

Catch 'em Early   About half the boys and girls mature physically before thirteen, so holding your discussion around age ten or eleven is usually a safe bet to beat the onset of puberty changes. However, puberty changes in both boys and girls can begin as early as seven. The best approach to correct timing is to look for the early indicators that puberty is imminent. Usually girls begin their menstrual cycle about eight months after their breasts develop. On the average, boys have their first ejaculation one and a half to two years after their voices change and their pubic hair thickens.

You want to monitor your child's growth in order to allow yourself time for discussion, especially if you have an early bloomer. But don't delay your discussion past age eleven, even if you have a late-maturing child. Puberty and its ramifications will be a frequent topic among your child's friends and he or she is entitled to be well versed on the subject, even if his biological clock is running slow.

Plan Your Talk   Your research will uncover a wide range of topics appropriate to adolescent training. Limitations of time and interest require that you restrict your remarks to cover only a fraction of the topics you might want to address. While choice of topics is really a matter of personal preference, the following topics seem most relevant:

Physical changes. Tell your children that they can expect rapid growth shortly. Be sure to tell your boys that girls usually begin their growth spurt ahead of males. Both boys and girls will need additional sleep and better nutrition to renew their strength and energy. Changes in the sex organs will coincide with rapid growth: The penis and testicles will enlarge and breasts will develop. Plan to stress the fact that the size of these organs is biologically determined and is in no way related to their sexual performance or their ability to bear children. A full explanation of the menstrual cycle is needed well before girls begin their first period. In addition to the facts, build your daughter's confidence and excitement about the prospect of beginning her menstrual cycle.

All children are on different biological timetables. Some will mature early and some late. It is possible that your son or daughter can still be a child at age twelve or thirteen. The psychological implications of late development are staggering. Your job is to provide the necessary reassurance and encouragement as your late-blooming children struggle to fit in with their more mature friends. Underscore the fact that being late in developing is normal for some people and that nothing is physically wrong.

Sexual responsibility. Hopefully, you have already laid the groundwork here, having covered the rights of others regarding sexual behavior and the need to limit sexual involvement before marriage. If not, by all means cover these items now!

While we are planning to tell Keri and Jimmy that we expect them to follow specific rules regarding their sexual conduct, we know the decision to comply with these rules ultimately must be theirs. As they enter puberty, our control over their actions will fade. In the final analysis, it will be their choices, not ours, that will determine their sexual behavior. Knowing this, we have decided to address the topics of premarital sex, contraception, and sexually transmitted diseases when presenting our guidelines for sexual morality. Of course, the discussion of sexual conduct requires a more elaborate dialogue than can be presented here. The complexity and seriousness of the subject precludes our providing a truly realistic example. Nevertheless, here is the gist of what we are likely to say about sexual conduct, using our DIFFER format:

"You'll soon be capable of conceiving children [description statement]. We think you're probably aware that pregnancy could occur if you have sexual intercourse, and we suspect you don't want that to happen [interpretation statement]. To be honest, we have mixed feelings about discussing premarital sex and related topics with you because we don't wish to appear as if we're encouraging it. We think pregnancy is a very serious matter and we believe premarital sex is morally wrong [feeling statement]. Our strong feelings have led us to formulate three practices governing sexual behavior that we'll expect you to follow as a young adult: (1) deemphasize sexuality in your relationships—choose activities that promote friendship; (2) confront those who make sexual advances with your belief that sexual involvement is progressive, always leading to further involvement, and tell them of your decision not to fall into this trap; (3) save your body for the person you'll eventually marry.

"We know your friends will be talking to you about sex, and some of your friends will want you to break with the three rules we want you to follow [effect statement]. Because you need to be fully informed regarding premarital sex and sexually transmitted diseases in order to commit yourself to your family's position, here are the facts we think you should know [result statement]."

Before leaving the subject of sexual responsibility, we plan to tell our children that they can expect to experience sexual tension as a result of the production of new chemicals in their bodies. We want them to know they will develop an appetite for sex, just as they have an appetite for food. They will need a way to release this tension. If long walks and cold showers provide a satisfactory outlet, fine. But we don't want them to develop guilt feelings over something as normal as masturbation. Having already addressed masturbation in early childhood, Keri and Jimmy should be comfortable discussing the subject as adolescents.

A preteen needs to hear that being sexually responsible means managing his or her fantasy life, particularly as it relates to masturbation. Spontaneous erotic reactions are normal. Self-generated erotic fantasies are another matter. We want our children to know that use of sexually explicit magazines and so-called adult television to simulate sexual fantasies is morally wrong. Pornographic material is demeaning and exploitative. Its use cheapens sex. It undermines sex in marriage, causing its victims to visualize pornographic images when they should be visualizing the face and body of their loving spouse. Jesus cautioned, "But I tell you that anyone who looks at a woman lustfully has already committed adultery with her in his heart" (Matthew 5:28 NIV).

Being sexually responsible means controlling our conscious thoughts, since our conscious thoughts are part of our actions. Although the difference between spontaneous and self-generated feelings is subtle, parents need to draw the distinction for their children.

Inferiority and conformity. In chapter 6, "Building Self-Esteem," we sought to establish the link between feelings of inferiority and acts of conformity. Adolescence intensifies feelings of inferiority, thereby increasing teenagers' need to conform. Early adolescents must cope with rapid growth and hormonal changes, new and strange emotions, and the growing importance of their friends and what they think. The judgments of their peers reign supreme. Early adolescents quickly come to the conclusion that their popularity depends on how well they live up to their peers' standards regarding clothes, food, movies, music, and language.

Preteens need to know that the advent of puberty can put at risk their ability to think and act independently. Before these drastic changes in perspective occur, parents should present family rules relating to alcohol and drugs. Our planned remarks on alcohol and drugs will closely follow our remarks about sexual behavior (see above). Probably we will use our DIFFER format to say something like this:

"Soon lots of the kids you know will be drinking alcohol and taking drugs [description statement]. You're probably wondering what's wrong with trying these things just once [interpretation statement]. But we want you to know that we're concerned and worried about the damaging effects of alcohol and drugs. Your using them would greatly upset us. Our strong feelings have led us to formulate three rules regarding alcohol and drug use: (1) no illegal drugs—period; (2) no misuse of prescription or over-the-counter drugs—that means no use of drugs to lose weight, build muscles, sleep, stay awake, or relax; (3) no use of alcohol—period. We know it will be hard to say no if everyone else is drinking and doing drugs [effect statement]. To help you comply with our family rules, here are the facts of alcohol and drug abuse [result statement]."

Confusion and the search for identity. Preteens need to be told it is likely they will question many of the family's practices and routines during adolescence. For example, it is not unlikely that suddenly they will stop eating breakfast so they can shower and fix their hair before school, or they'll stop attending church activities, preferring to stay in their rooms and listen to music. They will become as confused as their parents about the new people they are becoming. They will be pulled in many directions, for sure.

While these changes will be disturbing, parents need to communicate to children that they are perfectly normal and natural. More important, parents need to assure their preteens that they will continue to love them despite their frequent mood changes and contradictory behavior. Finally, preteens need to know that the turmoil they will be experiencing won't last forever. They will emerge as stable adults.

Drawing away from the family. Tell your preteen that to become an adult he must shift from a dependent to an independent relationship with his family. This process often takes ten or more years, and sometimes it may never be completed. The process begins by his feeling uncomfortable being with the family. Assure your preteen you know he is not ashamed of the family but rather is embarrassed by the child-adult role that is no longer appropriate. Tell him you will respect his attempts to avoid being seen in public with the family. Recognize the fact that his friends will become increasingly important to him, and assure him you will respect his need to spend more and more time away from the family. Encourage him to work a job and participate in school activities in order to develop increased competence and confidence.

Emphasize the relation between freedom and responsibility. As your teens become more responsible, increase their freedom. However, don't grant complete freedom until your children are self-sufficient. Insist that they always tell you where they are going and with whom. Establish curfews for school nights and weekends, with exceptions for school proms, cast parties, and so on. Determine what is off-limits, what places you don't want your kids to be: teenage hangouts, video arcades, convenience stores. Never accept the argument, "Everybody else's parents let them blah, blah, blah!" Remind them that you are not everybody else's parents.

Preparing for Adulthood

As the confidence and self-esteem of older adolescents start to grow, they begin to ponder serious questions: What will I do after I finish high school? How can I support myself? Where will I live? When should I marry? Who should I marry? Just as you went away with your preadolescent to hold a series of discussions, plan to invite your now preadult to join you in another round of talks. Those talks should address the following topics:

Love and Marriage Your seventeen- or eighteen-year-olds probably have fallen in and out of romantic love several times since becoming adolescents. They have found someone of the opposite sex and become a couple, spending every spare moment together staring into each other's eyes. There is no feeling quite like it. But then the excitement and thrill began to fade. Minor differences led to harsh words and icy insults. Resentment built up. After two or three unsuccessful reconciliations, they broke up. These failed relationships should have taught your preadults an invaluable lesson: Lasting love is more than a feeling—it is a commitment to care for another person as much as you care for yourself.

Now is the time to drive home this invaluable lesson. Although the truth of which we speak probably is beginning to dawn on your preadult, spell it out in capital letters. Remind him or her that the Bible describes marital love as a man and woman becoming "one flesh." Two actually become one. That means what one marriage partner does for the other, he does for himself.

If Eric makes the evening meal and does the dishes afterward because Linda is tired, he takes satisfaction in the fact that Linda has had a chance to relax, because Linda is a part of him. It's as if our marriage were a person pumping water, Linda acting as our right arm and Eric our left. When the right arm gets tired, the left arm willingly takes over. The left arm never says, "Hey, I pumped last night; it's your turn to pump." Instead, the left arm pumps away until the bucket is full because it is part of the body whose thirst will be quenched by the water pumped. Lasting love is sacrificial. In marriage, partners sacrifice their individual interests for the good of their union.

We plan to recommend to Keri and Jimmy that they test the love they feel for the person they plan to marry. A long courtship of a year or more will help them to know their true feelings. The sacrificial love they will need to make their marriages work should be evident over an extended courtship. Premarital counseling with a certified marriage counselor before announcing their engagement will provide a final check on their ability to love sacrificially.

Choosing a Career   Part of Eric's duties as a college professor is to advise freshmen students. He is alarmed that so many young people have no concept of the world of work. Not having chosen a career at age eighteen is fine, but not knowing what the career choices are at that age is cause for concern. We plan to explain to Keri and Jimmy that the work world consists of people who work with numbers, words, other people, and/or things. At age eighteen, Keri and Jimmy should have a pretty good idea of their interests and skills.

Usually a person's interests and skills are closely correlated: A person who is interested in numbers is usually good with numbers, and vice versa. We will ask Keri and Jimmy to share their perceived strengths and compare their perceptions to ours. If we agree, we'll put them in touch with as many people as possible whose work involves their interests and skills.

If Keri is interested in numbers, for example, we'll have her talk to the accountants, actuaries, engineers, math teachers, statisticians, and computer programmers we know. We'll suggest that she take them to lunch and visit their workplace afterward. The object is for her to learn about that part of the world of work for which she is best suited. Once enlightened, Keri will be in a much better position to determine the amount of additional education she needs, where she's going to get that education, what she'll study, and the jobs she'll seek after completing her education.

Money We believe it is our responsibility to teach our children Christian attitudes toward money and the pursuit of money. Jesus had a great deal to say on the subject. His main point is hard for our materialistic society to accept: Worldly riches and spiritual poverty go hand in hand. We intend to invite our children to think about how they are going to acquire and manage material resources during their lifetimes. We plan to suggest that they consider living on 80 percent of their net income, giving 10 percent to God, and saving the remaining 10 percent. If they decide to live on 80 percent of their net income, we'll invite them to consider how much money they'll need to earn in their first job in order to meet expenses. Then we'll encourage them to speculate on the size of their income five, ten, and twenty years after they begin working—and to speculate on what they plan to do with that money after meeting their expenses.

We will want to know when they plan to buy their first house, how much house they think they'll need, and why. How will they afford their first house? How will they afford their dream house? When will they want to retire? Why will they want to retire then? How will they want to live in retirement? Why will they want to live that way? How will they afford to retire when they want to, and how will they live as they wish in retirement?

Thinking about these questions will give our children the opportunity to develop life plans consistent with the teaching of Jesus. While much of their thinking will be preliminary and subject to change, they will at least have set goals to guide them in later decision making.

Leaving Home   More and more adult children are living at home after beginning full-time work. We want our children to assume responsibility for providing their own housing, once they begin work, in order that they become independent of us. We will ask our children where they plan to live after they begin full-time work. If they answer, "At home, why?" we'll ask, "For how long?" Hopefully, they will already be thinking about the need to set up housekeeping elsewhere.

While we want our children to leave home as soon as they are financially able, we want them to feel free to return home temporarily if they need emotional support or financial assistance. We plan to tell them of our interest in their welfare and willingness to open our home to them in the event of a crisis.

Parents should start early imparting life skills to children, modeling their values through their behavior and sharing basic principles during periodic teaching moments. It's a brick-by-brick task, really. But the basic truths by which parents live eventually will find their way into the minds of children. And what greater reward than to see your children successfully take on adult responsibilities.

8
Managing Friendship

Children's children are a crown to the aged, and
parents are the pride of their children.

Proverbs 17:6 NIV

Becoming Friends

As a college teacher, it is Eric's responsibility to objectively evaluate the work done by his students. In order to
remain impartial, Eric keeps his distance, insisting that
students follow the traditions which have separated students and teachers over the centuries: addressing him by
his courtesy title, Dr. Matthiesen; being punctual; meeting
deadlines. With many unspoken messages, Eric lets his
students know that, although he is friendly, he is not their
friend.

After graduation, things change. No longer responsible
for overseeing their education, Eric begins to relate to his
former students as colleagues, asking their advice, learning from their experiences, sharing books and articles.
Where there was distance, now there is closeness. Where
there was uncertainty, there is now confidence. Lifetime
friendships form.

Families too are better off waiting until parents have
done their job before establishing friendships. We know
couples who want to be friends with their younger children, treating them as little adults. These children are on
a first-name basis with their parents. When little Johnny
wants something he says, "Betty [that's Mom], give me
fifty cents. I want some ice cream." Betty (Mom) replies,
"Gee, honey, it's almost time for dinner. Don't you think

you should wait until after you eat before you have an ice-cream bar?"

"No," says Mom's little friend Johnny. So in the interest of friendship, Mom goes along with Johnny; Johnny learns that he can get his way by exploiting his parents' strange need for his friendship.

Around high school graduation, however, successful parents will have worked themselves out of a job, having turned out children capable of living on their own. Then both parent and child can work to form a new relationship, one based on friendship. Where before an independent adult cared for a dependent child, now two independent adults seek mutual interests, provide mutual caring, and lend mutual assistance. They share certain values and their life-styles overlap somewhat, but they are very different people.

Inevitably, significant differences will arise and threaten to undermine the redefined relationship. But if parents and adult children focus on areas of agreement and mutual interest, they can manage most differences. Tolerating each other's differences is critical to establishing and maintaining parent-adult child friendships. When sharp differences occur, parents must ask themselves, "How would I react to a good friend who thinks or behaves that way?" and act accordingly.

Unfortunately, some parents believe that once their children are grown, serious and intense involvement with them should end. That way there is little risk of serious disagreement. Parents who are superficial with their children need not fear rejection of their innermost thoughts and feelings. It's safer that way. But what a price they pay! They pass from mortal existence without having been understood and fully appreciated by their children. And they are easily forgotten. Fortunately, most parents prefer a deeper level of interaction with their adult children.

Staying Friends

Even if you are the best of friends with your adult children, problems are bound to come up from time to time that must be resolved or they will undermine your relationship. Although conflict is unpleasant, it is a natural and normal part of life. Every relationship of substance involves conflict and the feelings that result from unresolved problems: resentment, anger, frustration, and disappointment. While we can't avoid conflict and the negative feelings that result, we can effectively handle conflict to prevent damaging our relationships.

Conflict Resolution Styles

When faced with a conflict, parents and adult children have three choices:

1. *Accept things the way they are.* Suppose the parents of an adult child believed their son was taking advantage of their generosity by asking them to baby-sit for their granddaughter more frequently than they liked. If they chose to accept the status quo, they might say something like, "We don't like having our granddaughter here all the time, but I suppose there's nothing we can do about it."

2. *Exercise power.* If they decided to use force, they might say, "Either you stop asking us to baby-sit so much or we'll refuse to baby-sit at all."

3. *Negotiate.* If they decided to seek a mutually agreeable solution, they might say, "Let's find someone else to baby-sit and look for a way you can afford the additional expense."

Conflict Resolution Outcomes

Each of the above choices has definite results. Those who choose to accept things the way they are usually end up in a *win-lose* situation. In a win-lose situation only one party ends up getting what they want. The people who frequently find themselves in win-lose situations are those who operate from an either-or perspective. "Either our son gets the baby-sitting services he wants, or he'll get angry at us for refusing to baby-sit for our granddaughter," lament the accepting parents.

Those who choose to exercise power usually end up in a *lose-lose* situation. Their plight is ironic because their motivation for exercising power frequently is to obtain a win-lose situation. But most people defend themselves when others try to coerce them. They fight back, forcing the aggressor to compromise. When people compromise, usually neither side is satisfied with the outcome. "We don't like having to give up so many evenings to baby-sit our granddaughter," grumble the power-oriented parents. "We don't like our parents' threatening to refuse to baby-sit for their granddaughter," grouse the power-oriented children.

Those choosing to negotiate solutions to their differences usually end up in *no-lose* situations. Their goal in negotiating is to find a solution that meets everybody's needs. Hopefully no one will have to give up something they want and need. "We both need more time for ourselves," observe the negotiating parents. "Let's agree not to exchange birthday and Christmas gifts this year and use the money to hire a baby-sitter once a week for the next twelve months," say the adult children.

Although clearly negotiation is the most desirable means, few people use the no-lose approach to solve their problems. Its infrequent use comes as no surprise, since so many people are used to exercising power or accepting a bad situation. By far the biggest obstacle to seeking a no-lose solution is that the other party has to agree to negotiations before you can begin the process.

And since most people are more comfortable making power plays than negotiating, it is difficult to get others interested in the process. But there are some things you can do to improve your chances of successfully negotiating solutions.

Nine Steps to No-Lose Problem Solving

Keep in mind that each of the following nine steps is needed in a no-lose approach to solving problems.[1] Granted, the process appears mechanical as presented here; however, as you become skilled at applying each step to solving your problems, you will find that the structure becomes less obtrusive and almost second nature to you.

1. *Identify what is bothering you.* You know when you are angry, irritated, or frustrated. Your instincts tell you to lash out, to fight back. But when you do, you often find you cannot put your frustration into words. You feel that others see you as a "hothead," someone who explodes for no apparent reason. By carefully thinking about what troubles you before confronting the source of your frustration, you can avoid appearing volatile. If you think carefully about your problem, you might soon realize a fundamental truth about your situation: You own the problem.

That's right! You own the problem because you are the person who is dissatisfied. If your son owes you money and is not making payments, you are the one who stands to lose financially. Even if you are rich, you are the one who will feel exploited if the money is not repaid. If your daughter has not called you in several weeks or months, you are the one who needs to hear her news. And if you've heard all about what's happening in your daughter's life from your son, you are still the one who wants to be reassured that she cares enough to call you. Realizing that you own the problem will lower the role played by your emotions as you think about exactly what is bothering you.

2. *Find a good time to talk.* Timing is very important to getting another person to negotiate a solution. Remember, negotiation takes time. If your son or daughter is busy, tired, or frustrated, he or she will not be cooperative. Say something like, "Lately, I've been bothered about something that concerns you. When would be a good time to talk about it?"

3. *Share your problem.* By now, your son or daughter probably will know you are upset. What he or she won't know is why you are upset and how you want them to respond. Our DIFFER format (*see* chapter 1) will enable you to specifically describe your problem. The following examples illustrate how DIFFER can completely and accurately describe a problem you might be having:

"This is the sixth time you've asked us to baby-sit this month [description statement]. We're wondering if you've thought about how so many baby-sitting responsibilities affect our plans [interpretation statement]. We love you and want to help you, but we get irritated when asked to baby-sit so often [feeling statement]. When we say yes to baby-sitting, we often have to cancel our own plans [effect statement]. We would like to discuss with you some ways that you can get some time away from the kids without our having to baby-sit so often [result statement]."

"You've skipped the last four loan payments [description statement]. We're wondering if you're having any financial problems [interpretation statement]. We don't want to pressure you, but we feel hurt that our agreement is not being honored [feeling statement]. When you don't pay us, we can't pay our bills [effect statement]. We would like to find a way in which you can make your payments and still not be financially strapped [result statement]."

"We haven't heard from you in over seven weeks [description statement]. We're wondering if you're working too hard, or if you're having some kind of a problem [interpretation statement]. We love hearing from you, and we get upset when we don't hear from you [feeling statement]. When you don't call, we wonder if you still care about us [effect statement]. We want to discuss how you can keep in touch without having to take a lot of time away from your work or spending a lot of money [result statement]."

The use of our DIFFER format assures that your son or daughter will understand and appreciate your problem. Far too often parents and their adult children argue without ever trying to understand each other's thoughts and feelings.

4. *Allow for feedback.* Because conflict is stressful, there is a good chance that your son or daughter has not understood your problem. You can check on what your son or daughter has understood by saying, "I am not sure if I've fully expressed my thoughts and feelings. What is your understanding of what I've said?" This request tactfully invites your son or daughter to paraphrase your statement of your problem.

5. *Ask your children to state their needs.* In the interest of fairness, you need to know how your problem impacts on your children. In addition to doing the right thing by asking your children to state their needs, you stand a better chance of obtaining their cooperation. Usually, a simple way to get your children talking about their needs is to say, "Now, in regard to my problem, I need to hear what you want and why." Carefully listening to their replies is the hard part.

6. *Provide feedback.* Now it's your turn to paraphrase your children's needs. Try putting their thoughts and feelings into your own words. Carefully observe their responses and ask for clarification if you suspect they are uncomfortable with your interpretations.

7. *List as many solutions as possible.* Now that your children understand your problem and you understand their needs regarding your problem, you can work together to generate as many solutions as possible. A large number of solutions are needed to assure that you have not overlooked a good idea. That means you will need to accept every proposed solution as a legitimate possibility. It is important to withhold criticism at this stage so all will feel free to share their ideas.

8. *Negotiate.* Psychologist Thomas Gordon stresses the importance of everyone's being honest about the criteria they are using to evaluate the proposed solutions.[2] This usually means that each person puts his needs in order of importance. For example, parents might say, "We need to be sure that you're not taking advantage of us when you skip a loan payment. Sure, we want the money, but more important, we want to know that you're serious about your commitment to repay the money." Their son might say, "I need to know that you're more interested in my financial well-being than getting each payment on time." Rarely will parents and children be able to find a solution that will meet all their needs, but a candid exchange allows parents and adult children to search for a solution that will meet their most important needs. Everyone must agree to accept the negotiated solution. Majority rule is not a negotiated settlement.

9. *Check back.* What looks good in negotiation might not work in practice. Agree to discuss your problem and its mutually agreed-upon solution at a later date. It may be necessary to rethink your problem or find a new solution.

Of course, use of these nine steps in solving problems assumes that parents and adult children can cooperate to resolve their differences. What happens when adult children don't want to or can't cooperate?

Handling "Difficult" Adult Children

One of the thorniest problems facing some unfortunate parents is how to resolve conflicts with their "difficult" adult children. Under certain circumstances, the quirks we all possess become exaggerated. Some adult children emerge from childhood rigid, compulsive, antisocial, self-centered, unable to love, tense, manic, overambitious, or prone to compulsive striving. Their bizarre behavior leads to a diagnosis of neurosis. Negotiating solutions to conflicts with neurotics is extremely frustrating and often unsuccessful. Yet, parents of neurotics must find a way of relating to their adult children and make the best of a very difficult situation.

Suppose as an adult Jimmy becomes preoccupied with his own uniqueness and superiority, perhaps as a way of compensating for some deeply rooted insecurity or fear. Much of his communication implicitly demands that others enact a subordinate role in their relations with him. His communication typically contains an inflated view of himself. Many of his distasteful messages are really disguised demands for attention and recognition. He is low in empathic skills, unable to see the world through any eyes but his own. Finally, he often assumes prerogatives for which he will not reciprocate, demanding special favors but never extending them in return.

Acting in this objectionable manner, Jimmy might have the following conversation with Linda:

"I can't help Dad trim the trees in your backyard. I have a very important job, you know. I have a good reputation because I work extra hours. Putting out extra effort is important to my boss. Nobody ever worked weekends until I got there. All my performance ratings have been good because I go to the office on Saturdays. I've been with my company a long time, and I know what needs to be done. I want you to know that I've done a lot for you and Dad [not true]. I'll take care of you, but you've got to find someone else to help around the house."

Dealing with the difficult personality requires commitment and patience. Stressful situations produce "fight or flight" responses. Our instincts tell us to either avoid neurotic people or tell them off. Unfortunately, neither of these responses solves the problem. More effective solutions are needed. Together with his colleague John Hollwitz, Eric developed four alternative strategies for dealing with difficult people.

Direct Helping

Parents can use a straightforward approach to probe the underlying causes of their child's undesirable behavior. Using this approach, parents would directly question their child's motivations. In this approach, Linda would use our DIFFER format to confront Jimmy as follows:

"You talk a lot about being a success [description statement]. I am wondering if you're insecure about what you've been able to accomplish [interpretation statement]."

Perhaps she might suggest, as well, that he seek appropriate counseling. Although direct helping holds the best promise for a long-term solution, it is a difficult strategy to use. Instead of producing harmony, often direct helping can make the problem worse. For one thing, Jimmy might resent any reference to his psychological condition. Diagnosis and treatment are best left to trained specialists.

Linda's attempt at direct helping could cause Jimmy to enact further defensiveness and lead to further psychological consequences. Few parents have the skill or training needed to encourage their difficult adult children to acknowledge their undesirable personality characteristics.

Indirect Helping

Using indirect helping, parents deal with their difficult children subtly rather than through challenge. Parents exercise influence over their children by acting as a rational model. Take, for example, Jimmy's low-empathy comment, "I've done a lot for you and Dad . . . but you've got to find someone else to help around the house." His comment sought Linda's affirmation, which she should not give. Instead, she might respond with a statement such as, "Finding time to help others is difficult. I've had to make time to help your Aunt Sandy." This response undermines Jimmy's indifference without attacking him and risking a counterresponse. Linda's reply is noncommittal, and it is unrealistic to expect Jimmy to respond positively. But because the effects of indirect helping are cumulative, Jimmy might respond positively after repeated exposure to Linda's positive model.

Direct Coping

Direct coping is safer and perhaps a more effective strategy for dealing with a difficult adult child. Using this strategy, parents communicate strong supportive statements that recognize but do not challenge their child's insecurities. Rather than question Jimmy's need for recognition (direct helping), or model her own reasonable approaches (indirect helping), Linda would offer Jimmy positive feedback. For example, she might reply, "I'd be happy to consider the demands placed on your time, and

I appreciate your sharing your feelings with me. I can tell you're concerned about this problem." This response avoids evoking defensiveness and suspicion from Jimmy.

Indirect Coping

Here parents make no attempt to solve their child's problem. But "doing nothing" is by no means an easy strategy to follow. It requires a high degree of self-control in the face of abusive behavior. It is the strategy of last resort when the other strategies prove uncomfortable or unsuccessful. The strategy here calls for parents to maintain strict neutrality, concealing their annoyance to avoid further conflict. They anticipate unreasonable behavior and resign themselves to a distanced relationship in which they involve themselves with their children to accomplish tasks but seek no further involvement. While not the ideal solution, it is the only solution in certain situations.[3]

Actually, there are few ways to deal with difficult adult children, and each is hard to apply. But parents who employ a strategy appropriate to the level of communication skills they possess and the type of problem they face can minimize the impact of their difficult adult children and perhaps help them.

When parents establish and maintain a friendship with their adult children, they are opening the door to one of the richest relationships possible. Parents who approach their adult children as friends will enjoy the fulfilling experience of watching their sons and daughters come to terms with life and successfully manage on their own. Supportive parents accept the fact that their children might not live their lives as their parents lived theirs. In accepting the decisions their children make, parents get a fresh look at the world, seeing life as their children see it.

A Final Word

In his book *Family Forum*, Jay Kesler, former Youth for Christ president, addressed the fundamentals that make families succeed. Here are six characteristics of successful families adapted from *Family Forum* and applied to the concepts we have sought to present in this book.[1]

1. *Families succeed where love is openly evident between husband and wife.* We both regard Eric's mother as an excellent parent, yet she followed only about half the principles we've presented. "How," we ask, "did her children turn out so well?" The answer: She loved. She showed her affection for Eric's father by bolstering his ego, caring for his children, managing his home, and responding when he hugged and held her. Eric grew up secure that love governed his home.

We have talked about the need to touch, hug, and kiss children; parents need to touch, hug, and kiss each other too—in front of their children. Eric remembers the good feelings that swept over him when his father playfully kissed and hugged his mother: "Ah, things are good between my parents."

2. *Families succeed where respect for each individual is assured.* Parents communicate respect for their children by accepting them as they are. Parents whose love is contingent on the "when" message—"I love you when you keep your room clean, when you do your homework, or when whatever"—signal disrespect for their children. Parents communicate respect for their children by listening to their opinions and taking them into account by providing for their privacy, knocking before entering their rooms, and asking before they look through their things. Finally,

asking before using their property and honoring their requests not to use something can communicate parents' respect for their children.

3. *Families succeed where rules and boundaries are understood and communicated.* We have tried to underscore the importance of discipline to raising well-adjusted children. Boundaries communicate parents' love to children. Somehow parents need to get the message across to their children that when they say no, they are saying, "I love you." Children need rules to feel secure. Without control, children suffer from low self-esteem.[2] Successful parents balance control with love, and vice versa.

4. *Families succeed where problems are confronted openly and given proper weight.* We have sought to establish a link between using reflective listening and establishing intimacy. Children don't want parents to solve their problems for them, but they want their parents' support while they work through problems. Being there for your children bonds them to the family. We have also addressed the importance of resolving conflict with adult children. Unaddressed problems erode family relationships.

5. *Families succeed in homes committed to process.* We have not said enough on this point. People are continually changing and evolving. Children, in particular, change from month to month, sometimes even from day to day. Parents wonder, "What's going to become of this kid? Will he ever assume responsibility?" They forget that the jury is still out. Even when children are approaching adulthood, much hangs in the balance. Kids go through stages. Withholding judgment and not giving up on children gives them the time they need to grow and develop. It also does wonders for parental mental health.

6. *Families succeed where Christ is at the head of everyone.* It is hard for us to understand how people cope with the stresses of family life without Christ. Being able to leave

our problems with Him after a hectic day has gotten us through some pretty tough times. We pray with our children, and we don't mean those stock children's prayers, "Now I lay me down to sleep, I pray the Lord my soul to keep. . . ." We unload our troubles in language they can understand so they can see we are relying on Him for direction and support. When they have problems, we encourage them to take them to the Lord.

Eric's father has said the best years of his life were those spent raising children. The best years of our lives, too, have been those spent raising children. In the four years Keri and Jimmy have been our forever children, we have learned to open our hearts wider than we ever thought possible. The love they have expressed has taught us to love others more fully. They have forced us to meet greater challenges, to better cope with life's complexity, and to assume more responsibility. We adopted Keri and Jimmy out of our love of family life and a desire to grow in the direction that only the "path of parenthood" could take us. Writers James and Mary Kenny report that novelist Peter De Vries joked about this "path of parent-hood" when he observed that the amazing thing about marriage is not that adults produce children but that children produce adults.[3] Happy hiking!

Notes

Chapter 1 Using Effective Verbal Messages: The Right Mix

1. Adapted from Sherod Miller, Daniel B. Wackman, Elam Nunnally, and Phyllis Miller, *Connecting With Self and Others* (Denver–Littleton, Colorado: Interpersonal Communication Programs, 1988); *see also* Ronald B. Adler and Neil Towne, *Looking Out/Looking In: Interpersonal Communication*, 4th ed. (New York: Holt, Rinehart and Winston, Inc., 1984), 21–30.
2. Story and test adapted from William V. Haney, *Communication and Organizational Behavior: Text and Cases*, 3d ed. (Homewood, Illinois: Richard D. Irwin, 1973), 211–221.
3. Ibid., 221–228.

Chapter 2 Using Effective Nonverbal Messages: Great Performances

1. Nasim Dil, "Nonverbal Communication in Young Children," *Topics in Early Childhood Special Education*, vol. 4 (Summer 1984), 88.
2. Ashley Montagu, *Touching: The Human Significance of the Skin* (New York: Harper and Row, 1971).
3. Leon J. Yarrow, "Research in Dimensions of Early Maternal Care," *Merrill-Palmer Quarterly*, vol. 9 (1963), 101–114.
4. Edward T. Hall, *The Hidden Dimension* (New York: Anchor Doubleday, 1969).
5. Dil, "Nonverbal Communication," 92.
6. Paul Ekman and Wallace C. Friesen, *Unmasking the Face: A Guide to Recognizing Emotions from Facial Clues* (Englewood Cliffs, New Jersey: Prentice-Hall, 1975).
7. Dil, "Nonverbal Communication," 94.
8. Clara Mayo and Marianne La France, "On the Acquisition of Nonverbal Communication: A Review," *Merrill-Palmer Quarterly*, vol. 24, no. 4 (1978), 215.
9. Joel Alan Feinman, "Decoding of Children's Nonverbal Facial Expressions of Emotion by Parents and Nonparents" (Ph.D. dissertation, University of Massachusetts, 1982), 2.
10. Ibid., 84.
11. Judith A. Hall, "Gender Effects in Decoding Nonverbal Cues," *Psychological Bulletin*, vol. 85, no. 4 (1978), 845–857.
12. Feinman, "Decoding," 83.

13. Joel R. Davitz, *The Communication of Emotional Meaning* (New York: McGraw–Hill Publishing Company, 1964), 63.
14. Paul Ekman and Wallace V. Friesen, "The Repertoire on Non-verbal Behavior: Categories, Origins, Usage, and Coding," *Semiotica*, vol. 1 (1969), 49–98.

Chapter 3   Being a Parent Who Understands the Communication Process

1. This concept and view of the communication process is based on Dean C. Barnlund's Transactional Model in Johnnye Akin et al. (eds.), *Language Behavior: A Book of Readings in Communication* (The Hague, The Netherlands: Mouton, 1970), 47–53.
2. Ibid.

Chapter 4   Exercising Discipline

1. Disciplinary cycle adapted from Paul Hersey and Kenneth H. Blanchard, *Management of Organizational Behavior: Utilizing Human Resources* (Englewood Cliffs, New Jersey: Prentice–Hall, 1982), 149–173. Copyrighted Materials from Leadership Studies, Inc. All Rights Reserved. Used by Permission.
2. Range of abilities adapted from James Dobson, *Hide or Seek* (Old Tappan, New Jersey: Fleming H. Revell Company, 1979), 110.
3. Kevin Leman, *Making Children Mind Without Losing Yours* (Old Tappan, New Jersey: Fleming H. Revell Company, 1984), 23, 24.
4. Ibid., 46, 47.
5. Ibid., 70–72.
6. Ibid., 9–16.

Chapter 5   Establishing and Maintaining Intimacy

1. Tim Hansel, *You Gotta Keep Dancin'* (Elgin, Illinois: David C. Cook, 1985), 54, 55.
2. "Crisis, Stress Are Bound to Hit; Families Can Learn to Cope," *Omaha World Herald* (February 19, 1986), Metroextra, 1.
3. Norman Podhoretz, "Parental Commitment Tied to Teens' Problems," *Omaha World Herald* (February 19, 1986), 53.
4. John Rosemond, "Kids Get Too Much of What They Want," *Omaha World Herald* (May 9, 1986), 36.
5. Prudence Mackintosh, *Retreads* (Garden City, New York: Doubleday and Company, Inc., 1985), 45, 46.
6. Kevin Leman, *The Birth Order Book: Why You Are the Way You Are* (Old Tappan, New Jersey: Fleming H. Revell Company, 1985), 187.

7. Thomas Gordon, *P.E.T.: Parent Effectiveness Training* (New York: David McKay Company, 1970), 164.

8. James Dobson, *The Strong-Willed Child: Birth Through Adolescence* (Wheaton, Illinois: Tyndale House, 1978), 170.

9. Ibid., 168.

10. Gordon, *P.E.T.*, 63, 64.

11. Ibid., 59, 60.

12. Ibid., 41–44.

13. Dobson, *Strong-Willed Child,* 52.

Chapter 6   Building Self-Esteem

1. Lawrence B. Rosenfeld, "Beauty and Business," *New Mexico Business Journal* (April 1979), 23.

2. Mark L. Knapp, *Interpersonal Communication and Human Relationships* (Boston: Allyn and Bacon, 1984), 141, 142.

3. Rosenfeld, "Beauty and Business," 23.

4. Ibid., 25, 26.

5. Martha Weinman Lear, *The Child Worshipers* (New York: Crown Publishers, 1963), 225.

6. Pauline S. Sears and Vivian S. Sherman, *In Pursuit of Self-Esteem: Case Studies of Eight Elementary School Children* (Belmont, California: Wadsworth, 1964).

7. Paul H. Mussen and Mary C. Jones, "Self Conceptions, Motivations, and Interpersonal Attitudes of Late-and-Early-Maturing Boys," *Child Development,* vol. 28, no. 2 (June 1957), 243–256.

8. Mary C. Jones and Paul H. Mussen, "Self Conceptions, Motivations, and Interpersonal Attitudes of Early-and-Late-Maturing Girls," *Child Development,* vol. 29, no. 4 (December 1958), 491–501.

9. Sears and Sherman, *In Pursuit of Self-Esteem,* 177–207.

10. Jack Gibb, "Defensive Communication," *Journal of Communication,* International Communication Association, vol. 11 (September 1961), 141–148.

11. Inventory of defense mechanisms adapted from Ronald B. Adler and Neil Towne, *Looking Out/Looking In: Interpersonal Communication,* 4th ed. (New York: Holt, Rinehart, and Winston, Inc., 1984), 74–76.

12. Joel N. Shurkin, "Caution: Praise Can Be Destructive," *Family Learning* (May/June 1984), 29.

Chapter 7   Forming Values and Acquiring Life Skills

1. Jerome S. Bruner, Jacqueline J. Goodnow, and George A. Austin, *A Study of Thinking* (New York: John Wiley and Sons, 1956).

2. Grace H. Ketterman, M.D., *How to Teach Your Child About Sex* (Old Tappan, New Jersey: Fleming H. Revell Company, 1981), 37–51.

Chapter 8   Managing Friendship

1. No-Lose Problem Solving Steps adapted from Ronald B. Adler and Neil Towne, *Looking Out/Looking In: Interpersonal Communication,* 5th ed. (New York: Holt, Rinehart and Winston, Inc., 1987), 363–369.
2. Thomas Gordon, *P.E.T.: Parent Effectiveness Training* (New York: David McKay Company, 1970), 240.
3. John Hollwitz and Eric Matthiesen, "Communicating With the 'Difficult' Person: Organizational Symmetry in Turbulent Interactions," American Business Communication Association, *1982 International ABCA Proceedings,* New Orleans, Louisiana (October 1982), 55–64.

A Final Word

1. Jay Kesler, *Family Forum* (Wheaton, Illinois: Victor Books, 1984), 28, 53, 145, 225, 261, 388.
2. James Dobson, *Hide or Seek* (Old Tappan, New Jersey: Fleming H. Revell Company, 1979), 92, 93.
3. James Kenny and Mary Kenny, *Whole-Life Parenting* (New York: Continuum Publishing, 1982), 231.